THE SELF-RELIANT POTTER

Andrew Holden

Adam & Charles Black · London

Contents

Acknowledgements

I would like to thank my wife, Tricia, for her invaluable help in preparing this book. Without her, I would not have started, let alone finished it.

I would also like to thank Paul Hopwood, Carrel Jevons, the staff and students of Medway College of Design's Pottery Course, and the potters who generously supplied photographs and advice.

The cover photograph shows an earthenware butter dish by Suzi Cree, an earthenware tankard by John Reeve, and a stoneware teapot by the author (from the first firing of his power kiln).

Profile

Andrew Holden (born 1944) owns South Tawton Pottery, a small pottery workshop in the heart of the Devon countryside, just above Dartmoor. Here he makes a wide range of domestic stoneware and some porcelain. All the pots are raw glazed and once-fired in either a large oil fired kiln or smaller wood burning kiln.

In the last few years Andrew has done a small amount of lecturing. He has taught on the ceramics course at the Medway College of Design, and on courses and seminars in Britain, Holland and Germany. In the summer a workshop potting course is held at South Tawton, which is attended by enthusiasts from Britain, Europe and the USA.

Introduction

The glossy catalogues of the potters' merchants can be very seductive when it comes to selecting glazes, tools, kilns, and wheels, but these often cost a great deal of money, and buying materials ready-made will give you only a very superficial understanding of the craft of potting. This book introduces simple techniques which will allow you to avoid relying on pre-packaged glazes and equipment and to make pots that are truly your own.

The book demonstrates how to devise glaze recipes by simple tests and experiments, so that a real understanding of the nature of glaze materials is gained. Local clays, wood ash and other minerals can all be found for free, and these materials will provide you with unique and beautiful glazes.

Raw glazing saves time and money, but more important, enables you to make and glaze pots in a natural rhythm without the interruption of biscuit firing. As a raw glaze potter, you are never in the position of glazing ware made weeks before, for which you may have lost some of your initial enthusiasm.

Even modest electric kilns are expensive, and they are often thought second-best by their owners. You will be surprised how easy it is to build your own gas, oil or wood burning kiln from materials which are readily available. Using the plans provided in this book, it is possible to make a kiln which will suit your particular potting needs at a fraction of the cost of a bought kiln.

Wheels and tools are also costly, and you will find that you can achieve much and save a great deal with only minimal skills. Detailed plans and assembly notes are provided in both the kiln and wheel building sections of the book, and they are also illustrated fully with step-by-step photographs.

I hope you will find this book useful. I will have succeeded if it is found not on the bookshelf, but in the pottery with the odd clay thumb-print on it.

5

1 Understanding glazes

It is important to have an intimate knowledge of glaze, as this is one of the basic aspects of our craft. The mysterious liquids that are sprayed, dipped or poured onto pots bear no resemblance to the finished fired glaze, so to create the pot envisaged in the 'mind's eye' a complete understanding of the materials and what happens to them during the firing process is necessary.

In this chapter I am endeavouring to give background knowledge so that you have the confidence to produce original recipes from prepared minerals and from a rich source of locally found materials.

It is very pleasing to develop your own recipes, and it is also by far the most practical method of obtaining good glazes. There are many published glaze recipes, but testing them can be very unrewarding, as these glazes have been devised by potters for their particular kilns, and firing schedules. You will find only a small percentage of other potters' recipes will work really well in your kiln.

Armed with some basic knowledge you can easily adjust a glaze that seems to have some of the qualities that you require, but is not as yet ideal. Your ideal might be a more matt, a shinier, darker or lighter glaze and with a little understanding such a glaze can easily be perfected.

Sometimes, too, for no obvious reason, glazes that have worked well for years develop faults. With an understanding of how glazes work the faults of the problem glaze can be corrected.

First of all it is important to lay down the ground rules of glaze-making without bombarding a reader with over-complicated scientific terminology. I try to give a clear and uncluttered description of glazes, and in doing so I make a few sweeping generalisations. I feel this is for the greater good, as it is important to

Stoneware two pint teapot by the author, to which a variegated ochre glaze has been applied; the glaze breaks to a rich rust.

state the simple structure without all the 'ifs' and 'buts'. In my experience, people who have come fresh to glaze chemistry often feel intimidated by the technical nature of the subject, so the invaluable knowledge that is locked away in books on glaze chemistry is not available to many newcomers to potting. I hope this book will be a useful introduction for the newcomer to glaze chemistry. My intention is to enable the glaze experimenter to tackle more detailed books on glaze chemistry confidently.

What is a glaze?

Before discussing any of the finer points of glaze making, it is essential to define what basic ingredients are needed to make a pottery glaze.

Silica

Pottery glazes are made from silica which is the same material that makes all other types of glass, from milk bottles to windows.

Silica is a very abundant material, available to the potter in a pure form as ground flint or quartz. Many other minerals contain a proportion of silica (see table of materials, pp. 39–40).

Silica melts to a glass when heated to a temperature of 1700°C. As earthenware pottery is fired to a maximum temperature of 1200°C and stoneware and porcelain are usually fired to no more than 1400°C, the melting temperature of silica has to be reduced to make pottery glazes.

Melter

To use silica as a glaze at any of the various pottery firing temperatures it has to be mixed with a melting agent. This is known as a flux. It acts upon the silica to reduce its melting temperature to a level that can be used for glaze making. The most commonly used fluxes are: **calcium**; **magnesium**; **barium**; **potassium**; **sodium**; **lithium**; **zinc**; **boron**; **lead**. Some of these are available as pure minerals, but usually they occur in a composite form combined with other materials (see table of materials, pp. 39–40).

Sticker

The other main ingredient in a pottery glaze is alumina. This is used as a sticking agent, binding the

8

glaze to the surface of the pot and giving it some viscosity, which stops the glaze from running off the pot when it melts. Potters very rarely use pure alumina in their glaze recipes. It is usually obtained in composite minerals, such as feldspars and clays (see table of materials, pp. 39–40).

All pottery glaze-making works from the following principle:

A glaze is silica plus melters plus a sticker.

When making recipes potters usually work in this order:

fluxes   plus   alumina   plus   silica
(the melters)   (the sticker)   (the glassmaker)

To summarise we can say that to make a pottery glaze the glassmaker—silica—is modified by fluxes and alumina to suit the potter's individual requirements.

Glaze texture

Theoretically, a perfect glaze is a smooth shiny glass, which is thought of as having a perfect balance of fluxes, alumina and silica. This balance will alter depending on the firing temperature of the glaze. Stoneware and porcelain glazes require a lot less flux and more alumina and silica than earthenware glazes.

Matt or semi-matt glazes are those that in theory have an imperfect balance of materials. A glaze will be matt if there is too much or too little flux, alumina or silica. Consequently matt glazes are often referred to as alumina matt, silica matt, barium matt, lime matt, etc.

Glazes where one flux is predominant are often matt, as beyond a critical amount certain fluxes no longer cause the glaze to melt, but produce the reverse effect, stopping the melt and causing a matt glaze.

Glaze quality

Even when a glaze has a perfect, or near perfect, balance of materials its glossy surface has certain characteristics given to it by specific minerals. As these properties are by their nature very subtle I can only use such general terms as 'buttery', 'fat', 'thin', etc. to describe their appearance.

Wine jar by the author, glazed in a semi-matt yellow celadon. This glaze has a semi-matt surface because the recipe is slightly deficient in silica.

For example, usually earthenware glazes that rely on lead as their flux look 'softer' than borax glazes, which by comparison look 'brighter and glassier'. At porcelain and stoneware temperatures feldspar rich glazes have a 'fat' quality, which the Chinese call 'mutton fat'. This type of glaze does not run very easily, so it can obliterate any carved or sgraffitoed decoration that it covers. Used on the right pots these glazes can impart a generous quality to the finished ware.

Shiny glazes that have a dominant amount of calcium (from whiting, wood ash, etc.) appear much 'thinner and watery'. These glazes have a tendency to run, so can be ideal for sgraffito decoration, running into the cuts to create a greater depth of glaze and highlighting the marks. See photograph of Gary

Stoneware bottle by Jim Malone.
The decoration has been enhanced
by the fluid green celadon glaze
pooling in the sgraffito marks.

Standige's porcelain pot on page 44. I particularly like
these glazes, as at their best they produce beautiful and
interesting surfaces, the fluidity providing different
thicknesses of glaze, with varying depths of colour. The
main disadvantage of high calcium glazes is that their
fluidity means they are very susceptible to over-firing
but I feel they are so beautiful that it is worth risking
the loss of the odd pot caused by the glaze running
and sticking the pot to the kiln shelf.

Mature stoneware or porcelain glazes with a 'soft,
silky' or 'buttery' surface are usually associated with
magnesium, normally included in the form of talc or
magnesium carbonate.

Dolomite (which is comprised of calcium and
magnesium) will produce matt and opaque qualities in

most high-fired glazes. At their best these glazes are attractive, but the main disadvantage of dolomite glazes is that the surface is pitted with minute pinholes. If this type of glaze is used on tableware or ovenware the pinholes can make the pots very hard to wash up because food particles become trapped in the pitted surface.

Bone ash is comprised of calcium and phosphorus. When used in a shiny high temperature glaze the phosphorus may cause minute bubbles to be suspended beneath the glaze's surface, which reflect the light and give the glaze an opalescent quality. When a small quantity of iron is present in the glaze the reflected colour can be a subtle blue, known as 'chun'. Wood and other vegetable ashes also contain phosphorus and can give this opalescent quality to a glaze.

The various fluxes also have an effect on the fired glaze, reacting with any colouring oxide present in the mix to alter the colour of the glaze slightly. As the combinations of fluxes, alumina, silica and colouring oxides used in any one glaze are endless, the subtle effects of colour and texture that they give can only be fully appreciated by close observation of your results. The glaze materials section on pp. 38–40 also deals with the various properties held by different glaze components.

Glazes which have a balanced recipe with ideal amounts of alumina, silica and a wide range of fluxes, none of which are dominant, are by far the best behaved—they are troublefree and have a wide firing range. Alas, for my taste they are often the most dull. I feel that the craft potter's glazes are most interesting and beautiful when the texture may be described as 'rich and fat', 'limpid and fluid', 'silky' and so on.

Glaze thickness

The colour and texture of a glaze can vary considerably, depending on how thickly it is applied.

Very few kilns fire evenly; there is always a part of the kiln that is hotter or cooler than the norm. Similarly, when reduction firing there are usually parts of the kiln that are more or less reduced. Many pleasing variations can be gleaned from just one recipe by utilising the vagaries of the kiln. Over a period of several firings you will discover the most suitable firing

Bread bin made by the author, glazed in a fluid brown to ochre glaze. This pot has been glazed by pouring, taking advantage of the different colours and textures which can be achieved by variations in glaze thickness.

positions for individual glazes. An iron glaze of mine applied thinly and placed in the hottest part of the kiln where the reduction is also the heaviest gives a pleasing ochre glaze breaking to black. The same glaze much more thickly applied and fired several degrees lower gives a black to brown glaze breaking to red.

Over-firing and under-firing of glazes

During the kiln firing and cooling a glaze goes through several changes, and every glaze metamorphosis will be different. The melt during firing follows this sequence. The first part of the melt takes place when the kiln has reached at least a dull orange colour. This is when the glaze 'sinters', that is, becomes loosely melted together. As the kiln temperature rises, the different components interact upon one another and the glaze becomes quite active, boiling with small bubbles. If the firing is stopped at this point, the glaze is likely to be matt and pin-holed. At the glaze's maturing temperature the surface settles down and the pin-holes caused by the bubbling are smoothed out. If the glaze is over-fired it may start to boil again, causing a pitted surface, or more likely it will run, look too glossy, and some glazes may craze badly.

Over- and under-firing is often a question of aesthetic judgement. A fired glaze may be smooth and unflawed, but if it has been fired slightly below or above the usual temperature the subtleties that attracted one to the glaze in the first place may have been lost.

Pin-holing in the fired glaze is also caused by not allowing enough time at the firing's maximum temperature for the glaze to settle and fill in the pin-holes. For this reason many potters 'soak' their kiln, that is hold the top temperature for a time to allow the glazes to heal over. Usually ten to fifteen minutes is long enough to cure this problem.

Pin-holing can also be caused by trapped carbon in the clay body of the pot erupting through the glaze. A thirty to sixty minute soak at between 900°C and 1000°C will burn out the body carbon before the glaze starts to melt. Also see the section on once-firing, page 73.

Oxidisation and reduction

The quality of the atmosphere present in the kiln chamber during firing has a marked effect on the clay and glazes.

Almost without exception, earthenware is fired under oxidising conditions, where a clean non-smoky atmosphere is maintained in the kiln chamber throughout the firing.

Stoneware and porcelain can be fired under oxidising conditions, but high temperature firings also have the option of reduction firing. In the later stages of the firing when the chamber temperature has reached at least 950°C, and the glazes have started to melt, the fire is made to burn smokily, so less oxygen is available in the atmosphere. The hot unburnt fuel in the kiln chamber needs oxygen to burn, and it obtains this by taking oxygen from the glaze and clay materials of the pots, so that the chemical composition of the clay and glaze materials is radically altered. The reduction process therefore changes the colour and texture of the fired pots.

Reduction firing makes iron bearing clays become darker, and glazes are generally more likely to become opaque and soft-looking. For example, iron bearing glazes which are oxidised will give a range of colours from cream, tan, and various browns to black—whereas iron bearing glazes which have been reduction fired can produce greens, chun blue, pink, orange, red, ochre, brown and black. See the table of colouring oxides, p. 41.

Many potters who fire their pots in electric kilns and so can only fire their pots in an oxidising atmosphere try to imitate reduction firing, using the most tortuous methods. Even when they succeed in part, though, the results don't compare with the real thing. It seems preferable to concentrate on what may be achieved in electric kiln firing; there are many subtly differentiated oxidised glazes to be explored in earthenware, stoneware, and porcelain, where electric kiln firings can excel in their own right.

The author looking into his kiln. The flames are licking out of the spy holes during a reduction firing.

Glaze fit

In this section I discuss the common glaze faults and their cures.

Crazing

Glazes that are deficient in silica, or have potassium or sodium as their main flux have a tendency to craze. Crazing happens because the glaze surface is too small for the pot. As the temperature in the kiln is reached when the glaze melts, both the glaze and the pot expand. When the firing has finished and the pot starts to cool, the glaze contracts more than the pot, so the pot is larger than the glaze, and the glaze no longer fits it and crazes. To cure this problem the deficit of silica can be made up by adding either quartz or flint to the recipe. Test the crazed recipe with additions from 5 to 25%. This remedy may alter the quality of the original glaze, however, and if you want to keep its properties you may just have to accept that it crazes. In earthenware crazing will make the ware porous, but in stoneware and porcelain it can be very acceptable and is often used for its decorative quality.

When the crazing is caused because the recipe has potassium or sodium as its major flux, the problem can often be cured by substituting some of the material that is supplying the potassium or sodium to the glaze with a lithium material. Lithium has very similar fluxing properties to potassium and sodium, but it does have the reverse effect, countering the tendency of a glaze to craze. If potash feldspar, soda feldspar, or nepheline syenite are part of the recipe replace some of this with petalite or spodumene. If a high potassium or sodium frit is part of the recipe, as in some earthenware glazes, crazing can be rectified by replacing some of this with a lithium frit, often referred to as a 'low expansion frit'.

Shivering and shattering

Shattering occurs when the kiln cools and the glaze shrinks less than the pot, so that the glaze is too big for it. The pot is placed under stress as the interior glaze expands and pushes outwards, while the exterior glaze tears away from it. When the stresses are too great the pot shatters. This may happen in the kiln, when the pot is removed from the kiln or even some time afterwards. When pots are under slight compression, however, they may be strengthened.

'Shivering' is a less extreme effect which occurs under the same conditions; here, the glaze peels and flakes off the rim and edge of the pot.

Glazes which have lithium, calcium, magnesium or barium as their main flux are prone to shivering and shattering. This tendency can be cured by removing some of the above minerals and substituting potassium or sodium, which have high expansion properties.

Crawling

Dirt or grease on a biscuited pot may mean that glaze does not adhere properly, and peels away to leave bare unglazed patches on the pot's surface; this condition is called 'crawling'. But though dirty biscuit causes some crawling problems, most happen because particular recipes contain materials that are prone to this fault. Glazes which have a 'fat' quality when thickly applied are prone to crawl on firing, so materials which give this effect must be thought of as suspect. These are talc, magnesium carbonate, potash and soda feldspars and nepheline syenite.

Glaze materials that are too finely ground can also be the cause of crawling.

When packing the kiln, if you notice any hair-line cracks on the glaze surface rub them over with the ball of your finger, as they could open and crawl. These cracks usually appear only when the pots are bone dry —so if you pack the kiln with damp work the fault could go undetected.

Used with discrimination, crawled glazes, like crazed glazes, can have a quality all their own, and may be very dramatic.

Wearing properties of glazes

Glazes for non-functional ware can only be judged for their aesthetic qualities. Glazes for domestic pots must be not only beautiful but practical, and the only way to ascertain this is to use pots constantly in the home and observe what happens. Do the pots chip or break too easily? Do the glazes on oven dishes and casseroles craze when constantly reheated? Are the pots hard to wash up and becoming stained? Is the glaze surface hard enough? Does it become matt or scratched?

By its very nature domestic ware is used and abused, and the potter is failing if his pots do not meet the demands of today's household.

Making your own glaze recipes

Potters approach the making of new glaze recipes in many different ways. A favourite method is to adjust tried and tested glazes by adding colouring oxides and opacifiers. This is a valid method and with a little work will produce glazes that reflect the potter's individual taste, but although the glazes may be attractive they are rarely original, being based on someone else's ideas. It is probable that one will be merely going over ground that has been covered many times before.

Line blends

I have found one of the most rewarding ways of formulating new recipes is to make 'line blends'. Making a line blend consists of mixing two basic materials, or two separate mixes of materials to slip consistency. These are then blended together in varying proportions, giving a range of test recipes. (While reading this chapter it will be useful to refer to the table of materials on pp. 39–40, which lists the constituent materials present in the various glaze minerals.)

The usual method is a six-way blend of the two slips starting with six parts of the first material and none of the second, followed by ratios of five to one, four to two, three to three, two to four, one to five, and nought to six. For example, a stoneware line blend could be made of garden clay and potash feldspar. Both of these materials will contribute fluxes, alumina and silica; the garden clay will also give iron to the blend, which will colour the glaze too.

Line blends can be tested by applying them to small bowls, but I prefer to use small $1\frac{1}{2} \times 4$ inch tiles, which I make from a rolled out slab of clay. Each tile has a hole cut in it so when fired the complete range of blended tiles can be threaded onto a piece of string and hung on the pottery wall for easy reference.

If the blend that is going to be applied contains plastic clay (not china clay or coarse fireclay) the tiles need not be biscuited. The mixes can be applied to the raw tiles.

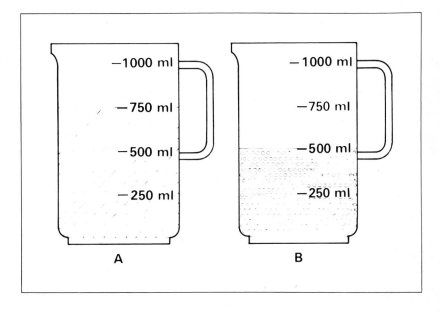

Line blend method

Weigh out a pound, or 500 grams, of each material.
These have to be separately sieved with enough water
to give them the consistency of single cream; an 80
mesh sieve will be adequate. As different materials
need different amounts of water to make them into
slips of the same thickness after mixing, a greater
volume of one material than the other will be produced.
For example, if you take 750 millilitres of the garden
clay slip (jug A) and 500 millilitres of the potash
feldspar slip (jug B) you will get an equal quantity of
slip from each material.

A one to six line blend would be conducted as shown
in Figure 2 (overleaf).

The blend is now completed. This is, of course, a
theoretical blend with imaginary liquid measures to
demonstrate the method. It may at first seem over-
complicated but in practice works simply and well.
Make sure that the various amounts of slip are
thoroughly mixed before dipping the tiles.

After you have worked through this method I hope
you will agree that it is very simple—inaccuracies can
creep in, though, if the quantities of slip are not
carefully measured, so be meticulous. If you are not
accurate results may be hard to repeat. For this reason
when I have an abundance of locally found materials
or when blending the less expensive bought minerals I
use larger quantities for my blends. If 3 lb (about 1500

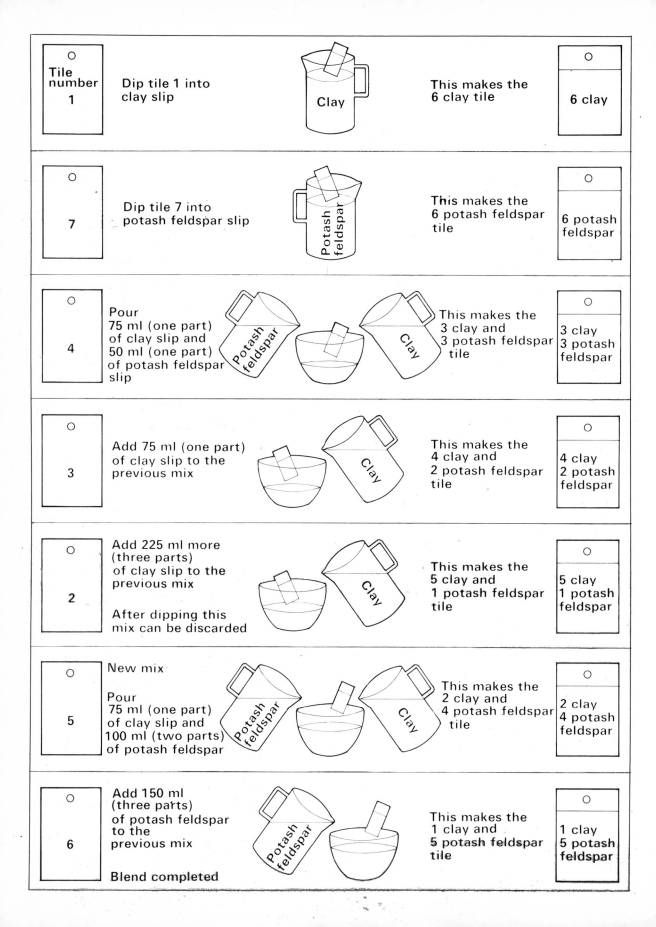

| Tile number 1 | Dip tile 1 into clay slip | Clay | This makes the 6 clay tile | 6 clay |

| 7 | Dip tile 7 into potash feldspar slip | Potash feldspar | This makes the 6 potash feldspar tile | 6 potash feldspar |

| 4 | Pour 75 ml (one part) of clay slip and 50 ml (one part) of potash feldspar slip | Potash feldspar / Clay | This makes the 3 clay and 3 potash feldspar tile | 3 clay / 3 potash feldspar |

| 3 | Add 75 ml (one part) of clay slip to the previous mix | Clay | This makes the 4 clay and 2 potash feldspar tile | 4 clay / 2 potash feldspar |

| 2 | Add 225 ml more (three parts) of clay slip to the previous mix. After dipping this mix can be discarded | Clay | This makes the 5 clay and 1 potash feldspar tile | 5 clay / 1 potash feldspar |

| 5 | New mix. Pour 75 ml (one part) of clay slip and 100 ml (two parts) of potash feldspar | Potash feldspar / Clay | This makes the 2 clay and 4 potash feldspar tile | 2 clay / 4 potash feldspar |

| 6 | Add 150 ml (three parts) of potash feldspar to the previous mix. Blend completed | Potash feldspar | This makes the 1 clay and 5 potash feldspar tile | 1 clay / 5 potash feldspar |

grams) of each material is used larger quantities of glaze slip can be made, minimising any small measuring inaccuracies. However, the average potter cannot afford to experiment with large quantities of costly materials such as lead frits, so smaller amounts have to be blended with great care.

Line blend into recipe

Most potters prefer their recipes to be shown in percentage form, so if a line blend gives a successful glaze you may wish to express the recipe that way. For example, the line blend may be made up as shown below:

	Parts
Earthenware clay	1
Potash feldspar	5
Total	6

Divide the earthenware clay 1 part, and the potash feldspar 5 parts by their combined total of 6. Then multiply the answers by 100 to bring them to percentages.

	%
Earthenware clay	16.6
Potash feldspar	83.3
	99.9*

*A six way line blend more often than not gives a recurring decimal place.

Line blend suggestions

The first glazes ever used (to my mind some of the most beautiful) were simple blends—mixes such as the limestone (whiting) and clay, and wood ash and clay that provided the early Chinese potters with their glazes. Simple clay and lead blends gave the European country potter his soft amber earthenware glazes.

To derive successful recipes it is essential to blend materials which together will give the three basic ingredients for a glaze, the fluxes, alumina and silica (see table of materials, pp.39–40).

The success or failure of line blends containing clay depend heavily on the type of clay used. I have often found contaminated clays the most rewarding, those, for example, which are found in the garden, river bank,

Figure 2 Line blending technique.

and so on. See section on local materials page 43.

When firing line blends or any kind of glaze test it is important that a strict note of the firing procedure is recorded and the maximum temperature is carefully noted, as when some good results are achieved it is important that they can be easily duplicated. A meticulously kept notebook can be a source for new lines of enquiry. Line blend permutations can be endless, but they are very worth pursuing—the effort put into them rarely goes unrewarded.

Line blend suggestions for stoneware and porcelain, 1230°C to 1300°C

Clay	+	Wood or vegetable ash
Clay	+	Feldspar
Clay	+	Talc
Clay	+	Basalt
Clay	+	Granite
Feldspar	+	Whiting
Feldspar	+	Dolomite
Feldspar	+	Basalt*
Feldspar	+	Talc
Feldspar	+	Wood or vegetable ash
Basalt	+	Talc
Basalt	+	Wood or vegetable ash
Basalt	+	Whiting

The following are suggestions for line blending two mixes of materials. By bringing several materials into a blend many more fluxes are introduced to the resulting range of test glazes. A combination of fluxes always have a more powerful effect in melting than a single flux, consequently one is usually assured of a good melt on several tiles along the blend.

50% Clay	+	50% Clay
50% Ash		50% Feldspar
50% Clay	+	50% Clay
50% Talc		50% Ash
50% Clay	+	50% Clay
50% Basalt*		50% Ash
50% Clay	+	50% Clay
50% Basalt*		50% Feldspar

* U.S. substitute for basalt could be VITRED, available from Hammill & Gillespie, P.O. Box 104, Livingston, NJ 07039 or Barnard clay, available from many pottery suppliers

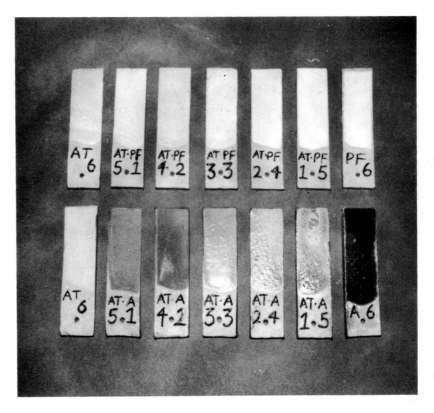

The photograph shows two simple reduction fired stoneware line blends. The top blend is a mix of iron bearing ball clay + potash feldspar. The ball clay is on the left and the potash feldspar on the right of the blend. The tile that has 6 parts ball clay and no potash feldspar, and the tile that has 5 parts ball clay + 1 part potash feldspar are warm orange in colour and will make good slips. The next three tiles have produced good usable glazes. These are also a pleasant orange in colour and have a slight gloss on them. The next tile is very different; it is 1 part ball clay + 5 parts potash feldspar, and produced a silky, slightly pink glaze, which makes me think there would be rewards in exploring the area between this tile and its neighbour, 2 parts ball clay + 4 parts potash feldspar. The 6 parts potash feldspar tile is a white over-viscous glass.

The second blend, a mix of ball clay and wood ash, has also produced several good glazes. The tile that is 4 parts ball clay + 2 parts ash has given a handsome dry yellow to brown. The 2 parts ball clay + 4 parts ash, and 1 part ball clay + 5 parts ash tiles are bottle green glossy celadons. These are good glazes but I feel they could be improved further by the introduction of another flux. As lime (a hard flux) is the major flux in these glazes, I would add a material that contains a soft flux, ie potash feldspar, nepheline syenite, petalite and spodumene. The pure wood ash glazed tile is a shiny bottle green glaze. Though pinholed it has a certain quality and demonstrates why ash is a favourite glaze ingredient with many potters.

The orange, yellow and green colours in these glazes have been produced by the iron present in the ball clay and the wood ash.

Line blend suggestions for earthenware, 1040°C to 1180°C

By adding 5% of whiting to the following blends the range of firing temperatures for any particular glaze can be increased.

Lead bisilicate	+	Clay
Lead sesquisilicate	+	Clay
100% Lead bisilicate	+	75% Clay 25% Flint
100% Lead sesquisilicate	+	80% Clay 20% Flint
Borax frit	+	Clay

I have found the use of lead frit and clay provides a most rewarding area for exploration.

Lead can produce the most beautiful earthenware glazes; at their best they are subtle amber colours. However, unless the glaze is chemically correct, lead (which is poisonous) can be leached out of the glaze, contaminating any food or liquid contained in the pot. It is *essential* that potters who use lead glazes for domestic ware have their fired glazes *checked before use*, and retested at regular intervals. One way of avoiding this problem is to use lead glazes only on the outside of pots and use a safe non-lead glaze on the inside.

When formulating blends for lead earthenware glazes I feel it is wise to start by using lead frits, rather than raw lead materials, as these can not only produce toxic glazes but are also poisonous in their unfired state. Lead frits are commercially manufactured mixes of lead, which are chemically combined with silica and alumina, and sometimes titanium. This process stabilizes the lead, making it a much safer material to handle.

There is no doubt, however, that raw lead materials such as galena (lead sulphide), and red and white lead do produce some of the most handsome earthenware glazes. If you are attracted to working with these materials do so with the knowledge that they are highly toxic. Don't let me put you off exploring this area, but first read all you can about the subject, and if possible talk to earthenware potters who use lead glazes about the problems they come across. Be aware that even a recipe that has been passed safe can produce toxic glazes if the glaze is at all underfired

Large red earthenware jug made by Richard Dewar. This pot was fired to 1180°C. A simple borax glaze covers a white slip which has been decorated by combing.

and not matured to a smooth shiny glass.

Copper oxide or carbonate must not be used in any type of lead glaze, or as an under or over glaze pigment on any part of a pot that could conceivably come into contact with edible substances. The copper will make even the safest lead glaze very toxic, as it has an 'unlocking' effect on the lead causing it to be very easily leached out when in contact with any acidic food or drink. See section on safety in the pottery, pp. 54–55.

Clay in glazes

Because I do not biscuit my pots, but glaze them in their raw state and once fire them the glazes I use for my own pots all contain large amounts of plastic clay (not china or coarse fireclay). The effect of the clay is to make the glaze plastic, so that the glaze is able to shrink with the pot, as the pot dries. A non-plastic glaze would flake off on drying. A glaze containing clay may be used on biscuited pots too. These glazes also have the advantage of not settling to a solid mass in the bottom of the bucket, as the clay helps to keep the whole glaze in suspension. It also gives the unfired glaze surface strength, making the unfired pot less vulnerable.

Learning from your results

After firing examine the line blends closely. Usually one or two mixes within a blend will look promising. Sometimes a more subtle blend is required between two of the mixes. For example, where an interesting result occurs from one part of the blend, one tile may be just too shiny and the tile next to it may be a little too matt, and a finer mix between these two tiles should produce the right result.

Sadly, sometimes the small area of glaze on a test piece will look very good, but when applied to a larger pot it is not so attractive. This may be because it is just the wrong glaze for the pot, or you may not have noticed annoying imperfections such as small pin-holes on the test tile. The glaze on the tile may have been of a different thickness from that which you applied to the pot, giving a very different result.

On the other hand, you might find that a test glaze which is uninspiring on the tile would look just right on a larger area. This is why I occasionally go back to my old tests and rummage through them. I have often found good glazes that I discarded the first time round.

One disadvantage of test tiles is that unless you examine the fired glazes closely it is hard to recognise runny glazes. These lie flat on the tile, but when applied to a pot will run. With luck this may give you beautiful results, creating changes of colour and texture, but often the glaze runs too far and sticks the pot to the kiln shelf.

After you have formulated a successful glaze, the recipe should be thought of as a base glaze. Many more glazes can be produced from it by adding various colouring oxides and opacifiers—see the list of colouring oxides and opacifiers, page 41–2.

Base glazes

Many potters are content to glaze their pots using other potters' glaze recipes. I feel that if the finished pot is going to be a sincere reflection of its maker's original concept a similar amount of time and effort should be spent on formulating the glaze as has been expended on perfecting the form. A glaze often coats most of the surface of a pot and contributes much to the visual impact of the work. If the glaze is not truly your own, the marriage between form and glaze may seem uneasy.

The following base glaze recipes should be considered as starting points for your own experiments. In some recipes exact materials are not specified—for example, where feldspar-type materials are required, the precise mineral is not given as these glazes will give good but varying results using any of the feldspar-type materials (potash feldspar, soda feldspar, nepheline syenite, spodumene petalite and Cornwall stone). When testing these base glazes your experiments can be extended by using colouring oxides and opacifiers. It is surprising how many glazes can be achieved from one base glaze.

A creative way of using established recipes is to line blend two similar glazes, which often produces a glaze superior to the two originals. A student I was working with showed me two rather undistinguished stoneware tenmoku test glazes. He did not want to abandon them, but he was rather at a loss how to make them a little better than the hundreds of other tenmoku recipes that are to be seen on studio pots. Not finding a better answer myself, I suggested line blending the two recipes. He hit lucky! The resulting blend threw up a glaze that was much better than its parents. Among the new glazes I have gleaned by this technique is an ivory white satin stoneware glaze from two ordinary off-white glazes. Blending two lead amber earthenware glazes together also produced a glaze which was better than the originals, softer looking and with a much wider firing range.

Look round the glaze buckets in your workshop. See what blends you can devise from your stock glazes. After a while you will develop an instinct for a winner. Be aware that blending two unalike glazes rarely works, but when it does, a truly new glaze is made which is nothing like its parents.

Base glaze recipes for stoneware and porcelain (1230°C–1300°C)

1	Feldspar type material	50%
	Ball clay	30
	Your choice	10
	Your choice	10

The permutations for making successful glazes from the above base recipe seem endless. A single feldspar-type material can be used or combinations of any number of these materials can be mixed, namely potash nepheline syenite, Cornwall stone, petalite, or spodumene.

There are numerous types of ball clay and the shininess of the glaze will be altered very slightly depending on which you choose, as the silica content of ball clays differ.

To complete this recipe add 10% each of two more materials (see table of materials, pp. 39–40). More fluxes are required to make a good melt and preferably a little more silica. As it stands this glaze is slightly deficient in silica so the more that is added the shinier the resulting glaze will be. If you want a high gloss then use a pure silica material, either flint or quartz. Amounts of whiting, barium and magnesium carbonate can satisfy the flux requirements, and wood ash and talc give both flux and silica.

2	Wood ash	50%
	Ball clay	25
	China clay	25

This is a dry matt glaze. The colour and texture will depend upon whether it is fired under oxidising or reducing conditions, and on the type of ash that is used. Particularly in oxidising firings, rewarding results can be obtained if red earthenware clay is used instead of the ball clay.

Additions of various colouring oxides will give interesting results. Cobalt and yellow ochre are especially worth investigating. This recipe can also be successfully used as a coloured slip under shiny glazes or those having a slight gloss (see photograph, page 30).

3	Potash feldspar	70%
	Ball clay	30

This glaze is best fired under reduction conditions. The resulting colour will be white to pink if a white ball clay is used, and pink to bright red if a ball clay containing iron is used. This glaze has come to be known as a 'shino type' in the West.

4	Red earthenware clay	45%
	Whiting	25
	Quartz or flint	20
	Any feldspar-type material	10

The above recipe will give a good clear glaze with a slight gloss in oxidising and reduction firings. Additions of more quartz or feldspar-type material will give a shinier result, as this recipe is slightly starved of silica. The red clay contributes some iron, and additional amounts will give a wide range of colours.

5	Ball clay	35%
	Whiting	25
	Any feldspar-type material	10
	Quartz or flint	25
	Talc	5

When fired this glaze is very similar to recipe 4. If a white ball clay is used it will be a clear uncoloured glaze suitable for the addition of 5% to 10% of zirconium oxide to make an opaque white glaze. Otherwise additions of colouring oxides will produce very similar results to recipe 4.

6	Red earthenware clay	30%
	Ball clay	30
	Whiting	30
	Magnesium carbonate	10

This glaze is best fired in reducing conditions where it gives a pleasant yellow to ochre matt glaze.

Base glaze recipes for earthenware, 1000°C to 1080°C

| 7 | Lead bisilicate | 70% |
| | Clay | 30% |

8	Lead sesquisilicate	75%
	Clay	20
	Flint	5

The above glazes are shiny traditional-looking lead amber glazes. If they are made up with a plastic clay they can easily be applied to raw pots and once-fired. The traditional country potter used the same clay in his glaze as he used to make his pots. The red earthenware clays of North Devon and Staffordshire contribute a certain amount of iron to the glaze, enriching its amber colour.

Suzie Cree's 1040°C to 1100°C honey glaze recipe is the same as base glaze recipe 7, with the addition of Cornwall stone and two parts whiting. For her glaze she uses a local red earthenware clay.

Further experiments with these glazes can be conducted using varying amounts of colouring oxides (see table of colouring oxides, page 41). Also 5% to 10% additions of flint and whiting can extend the firing range of these glazes and give the surface a higher and harder gloss. Obviously the quality of the glaze will depend very much on the clay body to which the glaze is applied, your exact firing temperature and the nature of the firing cycle of your particular kiln (see safety notes on page 55).

Stoneware cider jar made by the author. This jar was glazed with base recipe 2, which was combed. Base recipe 4 was then applied (to which iron oxide had been added). The result was a yellow ochre glaze showing a red line decoration where the underglaze had been wiped away. See section on decorating, p. 68.

The plus and minus game

As you have probably found out by now, glaze tests are often tantalising, producing glazes that are for one reason or another not quite ideal. The desired glaze may look promising, but have some small fault, being a little too matt, shiny, crazed, pinholed, etc. I feel the mistake many potters make is to disregard such results in frustration; to develop recipes that are truly your own, you have to look again at the failures and search for signs of 'life'.

For me, there are two viable methods of making the also-rans into winners. The first is to examine the recipe by the molecular formula method, which shows the exact proportions of the different glaze ingredients. This method is ideal—as at a glance you can see if the recipe is deficient or over-abundant in any of its constituents. The main disadvantage of this method is that the chemistry and mathematics involved frightens away the average glaze tester. Another problem is that the chemical formulae for such vital ingredients as garden clays, ash and other local materials are often not available. I have found the 'plus and minus game' a rewarding method of refining new glazes; it relies on examining closely the fired test and the written recipe, and doing a little elementary detective work.

First, leave the test piece around the workshop for a few days. Look at it every so often, decide what looks promising and what are its faults. Then write out the recipe in detail showing what each glaze material is contributing in the way of melter, sticker and glassmaker. You are able then to look for clues as to why the test glaze has acted in that particular way.

Example 1
For this example I have used a sycamore wood ash and local ball clay recipe.

Recipe A
Ball clay	33%
Sycamore wood ash	66

The glaze was fired to 1300°C in a reduction firing. It proved to be a deep bottle green thinning to light yellow on the test's edges, but where it was thickly applied some areas bubbled, giving it a porridge-like surface—an annoying fault on a handsome glaze.

The ball clay in the recipe contributes mainly alumina and silica to the melt. The ash is giving calcium (a melter) and silica plus very small amounts of alumina and some other melting agents. If the recipe is written out in detail it's possible to make some educated guesses about how to adjust the glaze.

Recipe detail

		Fluxes present	Alumina present	Silica present
Ball clay	33%	only small amounts	yes	yes
Sycamore wood ash	66%	Calcium plus small amounts of others	very small amounts	yes

When considering what the materials contribute to the glaze several conclusions may be reached. My best guess was that as only one main flux was present in the glaze. This was why an imperfect melt had taken place, causing the porridge-like texture on the test. So the thing to do is to introduce a secondary melter from the table of materials. I chose to introduce granite to the glaze, which contributes the melters, potassium calcium and sodium and also adds alumina and silica.

Bringing a material such as granite with its many components to a glaze sets up several complicated interactions between the glaze constituents during the firing, and brings about a much more fluid melt.

To ascertain the amount of granite needed in the recipe a line blend was made between the original recipe and the granite. As I did not wish to alter the original glaze radically only a small amount of granite was introduced to the recipe. I mixed up two batches of glaze for blending.

Recipe B

Ball clay	25%
Sycamore wood ash	50
Granite	25

The two recipes were blended in a six way line blend (as shown on page 20) and fired.

The resulting glazes were all similar to the original, but there were subtle variations in their brightness and texture. A test tile from the middle of the new blend was the mix that went into my recipe book. This was almost the same colour as the original glaze, but a little shinier and smooth with no rough spots.

Granite was my personal choice. I could just as easily have chosen any material that would contribute melters, such as basalt, potash or soda feldspar, nepheline syenite, Cornish stone, petalite, or spodumene.

Example 2

When the base glaze recipe 4 on page 29 is made with earthenware red clay and potash feldspar it becomes a very pleasant 'tea dust' brown when fired between 1280° and 1300°C in both reduced and oxidised firings. I felt that for some domestic ware it would be an advantage for the glaze to be a little shinier.

Recipe detail

		Fluxes present	Alumina present	Silica present
Red earthenware clay	45%	Calcium*	Yes	Yes
Whiting	25%	Calcium		
Quartz	20%			Yes
Potash feldspar	10%	Potassium	Yes	Yes

*Red clays usually contain calcium and small amounts of other fluxes.

The above glaze recipe would not seem to be deficient in flux, silica or alumina. The only guess I could make was that the recipe has a lot of calcium in it, and glazes that have an over-abundance of calcium are always matt (see page 38); over a certain amount calcium's melting power diminishes dramatically. The glaze also looked as though it might be too rich in glassmaker as the red clay, quartz and feldspar were all providing silica. So I made up two recipes for blending. In Recipe A I decreased the quartz to 10 parts and the potash feldspar to 5 parts, thereby taking out some silica and a little of the potassium melter. (Later these proportions were converted to percentages given in the recipes below.)

In Recipe B I increased the quartz to 30 parts and

increased the potash feldspar to 20 parts so adding more silica and bringing in more of the glaze's second melter, potassium.

Recipe A

Red earthenware clay	45 parts
Whiting	25
Quartz	10
Potash feldspar	5

Recipe B

Red earthenware clay	45 parts
Whiting	25
Quartz	30
Potash feldspar	20

The resulting fired blend was somewhat unexpected but a great success. Recipe A which had less quartz and potash feldspar was more matt than the original. Recipe B, with more quartz and potash feldspar, was bright and glassy. The blend gave a result somewhere between the two recipes, and it proved to my surprise that the original glaze was lacking in silica.

If the glaze had had enough or too great an amount of silica, adding more from the quartz and potash feldspar would have made the glaze far more matt. By adding more of the second melter (potassium) from the potash feldspar I was not relying so much on the calcium (whiting) to provide a smooth melt.

I now have three glazes from the blend which I use regularly in the workshop—the original silky matt, a smooth matt and a glossy version which I now use on my domestic ware.

	matt	silky matt	glossy
	%	%	%
Red earthenware clay	49	45	42
Whiting	27	25	24
Quartz	16	20	22
Potash feldspar	8	10	12

Although the texture of each glaze is different the new glazes still retain a lot of the qualities that I liked in the original. One of the most important things to come out of my labours is that I now feel I know this glaze intimately and should I need to adjust it some time in the future I can do so with ease.

I cannot guarantee that this method will be successful every time, but even when your hard work is not rewarded, useful information is always gleaned, from which a further and hopefully more successful test can be made. Practised regularly, this way of glaze testing will make you increasingly aware of glaze structure and after a while your educated guesses will become very accurate.

Fluxes (melters)

If you wish to bring another flux to a stoneware or porcelain glaze recipe it is best to introduce one that is radically different, as a completely new material in the melt will act more powerfully. For example, if you want to adjust a recipe that contains calcium and magnesium, both 'hard' melters, it is best to introduce a 'soft' melter or melters, such as potassium, sodium or lithium.

The main earthenware glaze fluxes, lead and borax, will always provide a good melt as long as the amounts are correctly proportionate to the alumina and silica. Small amounts of other fluxes are often introduced into earthenware glazes, which can have the effect of broadening the glaze's firing range and giving it a harder-fired surface.

Slips

Slips not only increase the range of colours and textures for any given glaze, but mean that decorative techniques such as sgraffito combing, wiping, and so on are possible.

The thickness of a slip is very important. If it is applied thinly by dipping or brushed on, a slip can modify the resulting glaze colour very slightly. A thick application will completely change the glaze. For example, in a reduction stoneware firing a transparent colourless glaze applied over a thick application of dark-brown slip will usually produce a medium green to bottle-green celadon glaze.

The darker coloured clay bodies will darken any glaze that is applied over them. A slip is essential to achieve some of the lighter colour glaze effects. An application of white slip on a red earthenware clay will, for example, produce a soft amber glaze rather than a dark-treacle brown from a traditional lead

Brown and white slips applied to test tiles and bowls.

glaze. Often a mundane glaze will come to life over a slip.

To derive the greatest varieties of colours and textures from tests, it is important that at least two different slips are applied to each tile or bowl.

Slips for earthenware, stoneware and porcelain

White slip
| White ball clay | 60% |
| China clay | 40% |

Should your potting clay be more or less plastic than average, increase or decrease the ball clay content as required.

White slip can also be used as a base slip to which oxides can be added to give a whole range of coloured slips (see table of colouring oxides, page 41).

When fired, slips do not melt to the same extent as a glaze, so any colouring oxide in the slip is not as easily dispersed as it is in a glaze. Three times as much colouring oxide is needed in a slip to produce a colour as would be required in a glaze.

Red brown slip
| White ball clay | 50% |
| Red earthenware clay | 50% |

Dark brown slip
| Red earthenware clay | 100% |

In stoneware and porcelain reduction firings a green celadon will become a red to black tenmoku when applied over this slip.

36

Local clays used as slips by themselves or mixed with china clay or ball clay often yield distinctive results. A few simple tests will indicate their possibilities.

Glaze mixing

To keep dust levels at a minimum wherever possible the weighed glaze materials should be added to water, rather than water added to dry materials. Glazes should be sieved at least twice. In the case of earthenware and stoneware an 80 mesh sieve is normally adequate. Porcelain usually requires a 120 mesh sieve.

Most glazes take a day to age, as immediately after sieving the mixture has not had time to settle down, and will glaze with an inconsistent thickness. See also the section on thickness of raw glazes, p. 60.

Large earthenware store jar made by Clive Bowen. The quality of the lead/clay glaze (fired to 1040°C) has been enhanced by using a white slip underneath it. This has produced a rich amber/honey colour.

Glaze materials

The table on pp. 39–40 gives a simple analysis of the most popular glaze materials. When creating a new recipe materials can be chosen that will satisfy the glaze's need for fluxes, alumina and silica.

Most of the fluxes are divided into two categories; 'soft' and 'hard', which is my way of expressing their essential characteristics. Generally the 'soft' fluxes are the more powerful melting agents and are used in stoneware, porcelain and earthenware glazes. The resulting glaze surface is softer and so more easily marked than where glazes have 'hard' fluxes as their main melting agent. 'Hard' fluxes have a powerful reaction at stoneware/porcelain temperatures where they can play a major role in the glaze melt, producing a hard durable glass. In earthenware glazes they can only be used as a secondary melting agent, but in this capacity they make an important contribution by increasing the hardness and durability of the glaze.

As well as having particular properties which establish them as either hard or soft fluxes, each individual flux has an effect on the quality and colour of glaze. What the effects may be depend upon the particular temperature to which the kiln is fired and whether it is fired under oxidising or reducing conditions.

I work mainly in reduced stoneware and porcelain where I have found that hard fluxed iron green celadons tend to be a yellow-green, whereas soft fluxed celadons are usually blue-green. Hard fluxed tenmokus break from black to ochre brown where the glaze thins, and soft fluxed tenmokus break from black to rust red.

A reduced iron stoneware glaze that has no hard fluxes in it and relies only on the soft fluxes, potassium, sodium or lithium for a melt can have very unusual properties. Whereas an iron glaze would be expected to produce a green celadon to a black tenmoku, in pure soft fluxed glazes the iron gives a colour range from a light pinky orange through to tomato red. A recipe for this type of glaze is given on page 28 (recipe 3).

An entirely hard fluxed glaze in reduction has a colour range of cream to bright yellow, depending upon the amount of iron present. A pure hard fluxed glaze will always be matt. See page 29 (recipe 6).

Table of Glaze Materials

Material	Flux (melter) present	Type of flux	Nature of flux	Alumina (sticker) present	Silica (glassmaker) present	Notes
Feldspar potash	√	Potassium	Soft	√	√	Melts to a white, 'fat' glass at 1250°C
Feldspar soda	√	Sodium	Soft	√	√	Melts to a white, 'fat' glass at 1250°C
Nepheline syenite	√	Potassium Sodium	Soft Soft	√	√	Slightly lower melting temperature than potash and soda feldspar
Cornwall stone	√	Potassium Sodium Calcium	Soft Soft Hard	√	√	Also known as China stone, stone, or Cornish stone. Melts to a glass at stoneware temperatures
Petalite	√	Lithium	Soft	√	√	See notes on crazing, page 16. A good starting point for glaze making as it melts to a pleasant glaze at 1250°C
Spodumene	√	Lithium	Soft	√	√	See notes on crazing, page 16. Does not melt so readily as petalite as it contains more silica, but still a very useful material.
Granite	√	Potassium Sodium Calcium	Soft Soft Hard	√	√	Melts to a fat glaze at 1250°C. Some are high in iron and will colour glazes.
Basalt	√	Potassium Sodium Calcium Magnesium	Soft Soft Hard Hard	√	√	Melts to a fluid glaze at stoneware temperatures. Its iron content will colour glazes.
Whiting	√	Calcium	Hard			Also known as limestone or chalk.
Magnesium carbonate	√	Magnesium	Hard			
Dolomite	√	Calcium Magnesium	Hard Hard			5% to 10% of dolomite in a stoneware recipe usually makes the glaze opaque and matt. Dolomite glazes are usually unsuitable for tableware as their surface is pitted with minute pinholes
Bone ash	√	Calcium	Hard			Bone ash also contains phosphorus. This can lead to the glaze having minute bubbles under its surface, giving it an opalescent quality

Material	Flux (melter) present	Type of flux	Nature of flux	Alumina (sticker) present	Silica (glassmaker) present	Notes
Talc	√	Magnesium	Hard		√	
Barium carbonate	√	Barium	Hard			Barium is a toxic material (see safety notes, page 55).
Zinc oxide	√	Zinc	Hard			Up to 5% of zinc in a stoneware or porcelain glaze can give it a clear bright surface. Above this zinc can cause pinholing and dullness.
China clay				√	√	
Other clays				√	√	See notes on clays, p. 50.
Quartz/flint					√	Pure silica
Lead bisilicate frit	√	Lead		√	√	Lead is used only as an earthenware flux.
Lead sesquisilicate frit	√	Lead			√	Compared with stoneware glazes, lead glazes have a soft surface, but I do not categorise lead as a soft flux, as its qualities are unique. See safety notes, p. 55
Wood ash	√	Calcium (mainly)	Hard		√	See notes on wood ash, p. 43
Borax frit	√	Various		√	√	Borax is a natural material containing the melters sodium and boron; it is a melting agent and also a glassmaker. As borax is soluble it is used in the form of a frit which is a commercially-made mix of borax, other melters, alumina and silica. The amounts of various materials in a borax frit depend on the manufacturer's recipe. Borax frits are particularly useful for producing bright, non-toxic earthenware glazes
Colemanite	√	Calcium boron	Hard			Colemanite contains the only natural non-soluble form of boron. Boron is unique as it acts both as a melter and a glassmaker. Colemanite can be an unreliable material, varying from batch to batch. Calcium borate frit is a reliable alternative.

Colouring oxides

The table below recommends the percentages of colouring oxides and the anticipated range of colours which will be produced from adding these materials. Very unexpected, interesting and occasionally beautiful results may happen when these boundaries are exceeded. For example, to obtain the usual range of purple to browns from adding manganese, the recommended quantities are 2% to 6%. However if up to 60% is added to a matt glaze a remarkable bronze to black glaze can be achieved. So think of these amounts as recommendations only—not as absolute limits.

Table of Colouring Oxides

Colouring oxide	Recommended %	Expected colours in oxidized firing	Expected colours in reduction firing
Cobalt oxide or Cobalt carbonate	$\frac{1}{4}$ to 3	Light to dark blue	Light to dark blue
Red iron	1 to 15	Depending on the type of glaze and the quantities used these materials will give the following range of colours:	
Synthetic iron	1 to 15		
Purple iron	1 to 15	Cream, brown, red and black	Green, blue, yellow, red, brown and black
Black iron			
Yellow ochre (iron)	3 to 30	(yellow ochre, purple and black iron are impure forms of iron and may also give speckling and other effects)	
Iron spangles	1 to 10	Dark speckles	Dark speckles
Ilmenite	1 to 6	Browns and speckles	Browns and speckles
Rutile	1 to 10	Tan to brown	Tan to brown
*Copper oxide or *Copper carbonate	1 to 10	Greens (Can be unstable, turns to a gas at 1250°C)	Pink, red, purple
*Manganese carbonate or *Manganese dioxide	1 to 6	Pink, brown, purple, and black	Brown, green, honey-brown, and black
*Nickel	1 to 4	Slate-blue, brown and green	Brown
*Chrome	2 to 5	Red, brown (only to be used at earthenware temperatures)	
*Antimony	2 to 5	Yellow (only to be used at earthenware temperatures)	
*Vanadium	1 to 6	Yellow	Yellow, blue and black

*These materials are potentially hazardous—see safety notes, page 55.

Stoneware teapot made by Mike Dodd. The pot has been raw glazed with a variegated runny bottle-green glaze. Wherever possible, Mike Dodd likes to use local materials such as low-firing iron clays, feldspars, and various wood ashes. In his words 'Some common sense, luck and experiment is for me the best and most reliable recipe – and great fun.'

Opacifiers

Opacifiers are generally used in transparent colourless glazes to give whiteness. They do not form part of the melt, but remain suspended in the glaze as small white particles. To make pure white glazes 3% to 10% of tin oxide, zirconium oxide or zirconium silicate can be added to a transparent base glaze. Titanium also has opacifying qualities, but generally makes the glaze creamy-matt or semi-matt. Additions of 5% to 10% are suggested.

Tin is expensive, but in some recipes there is no alternative. However, replacing the tin with zirconium oxide or zirconium silicate can often produce beautiful glazes, though of a slightly different quality.

While opacifiers are generally used to make white glazes, when used in transparent light-coloured glazes interesting and subtle results can be produced. For example, I have a transparent grey-green celadon glaze to which I added 10% zirconium oxide. This glaze is now a rather handsome grey opalescent celadon.

Adding opacifiers to a glaze can often cure crazing, although, of course, it will alter the colour of the glaze.

Any base glaze that has a tendency to crawl should not have an opacifier added as this will only accentuate the problem.

Using local materials

The garden and the countryside abound with superb glaze ingredients. Get to know the geology of your area—museum curators, geology teachers and mining engineers will be able to explain the local landscape and can not only tell you where to look but what to look for. Useful sources of materials can be found in places such as clay pits, brick works and quarries with stone-crushing plants, and you should find out where they are.

The most rewarding local glaze materials I have found have been local earthenware and ball clays, alluvial clays, granite and basalt dust, wood ash and iron slurry, but there are many others such as china clay, fireclay, fullers earth (a very plastic clay), limestone or chalk (whiting), hematite (iron), copper, cobalt, Cornwall stone, dolomite and flint.

Nowadays it is very worthwhile even foraging for relatively inexpensive materials such as whiting, as shipping costs make even the humblest materials costly.

Wood ash and other vegetable ashes

Wood and other vegetable ashes are a rich source of original glaze material. They are used mainly in a stoneware and porcelain glaze, though small amounts can be used in low temperature glazes. A disaster such as a burnt hay rick or barn full of straw can yield several hundredweight of valuable ash. The burnt trimmings after tree felling, or a bonfire at the local saw-mill will also produce valuable wood ash.

Ash is often slightly caustic, so it is wise to wear rubber gloves when preparing it. Don't do as a friend of mine did. He collected a plastic bucket of what he thought was cold wood ash from his bonfire. Left alone for a few hours this smouldered and caused a considerable fire.

To prepare ash as a glaze material mix it with water. Any charcoal floats to the surface and should be removed. If there is a large quantity this can be re-burnt. The remaining ash is sieved through an 80 mesh sieve and allowed to settle until the water content can be decanted. The whole process is repeated two or three times using fresh water on each occasion. This

Porcelain jar made by Gary Standige, glazed
in a mixture of local clay and wood ash. The
glaze is very fluid and has run into the
sgraffito, highlighting the decoration.

44

washes out any soluble salts in the ash, which can cause it to be an unreliable material.

Ashes vary considerably. Before doing any line blends or tests make sure that you have sufficient quantities available from a reliable source of the same ash. If not your efforts will be wasted. The local sawmill which is burning pine offcuts would always give a constant and reliable source of ash, and after devising glazes from such material you can be happy in the knowledge that the results are repeatable. But the small garden bonfire may give you only enough material to test your glazes and as there is no further source of identical material you may never be able to reproduce these. It is most important that you have a reliable source of ash for those glazes with a glossy surface, for any slight variation in the material will alter the result of the fired glaze. In dry matt ash glaze recipes and slips more variable materials can be used as the quality of the fired glaze is less easily altered.

The predominant materials in ashes are usually calcium and silica. The proportions of these depend on the type of vegetable matter burnt, the soil in which it was growing, and what time of the year it was cut. It is the trace elements in ashes that give these glazes their uniquely beautiful and distinctive qualities.

A typical analysis of a wood ash is given here, which should be used as a guide to the materials an ash contributes to a glaze. This rough analysis ignores the soluble materials that are washed out.

Calcium	up to 70%
Magnesium	up to 20%
Silica	up to 50%
Iron	up to 5%

Plus small amounts of phosphorus and other trace elements.

Sources of
local materials

Key

A School or college — Help from geology and chemistry teachers on how and where to find glaze and clay materials.

B Paint factory — Stone dust for glaze making

C Stone mason — Granite, basalt, marble (calcium) dust for glaze making.

D Woods or forest — Wood ash

E Stone quarry — Granite, basalt dust, etc for glaze making

F Brickworks and clay pit — Earthenware clay; secondhand fire bricks

G Saw mill — Wood ash for glaze making; sawdust for brick making; wood for wheel making

H	Your garden	Subsoil clay for either pot or glaze making. Wood ash for glaze making
I	Building site	Clay and sand
J	River and bank	Alluvial clay for glaze making; sand or grit for adding to clay bodies; yellow ochre for glazes and clay bodies
K	Electrician	Parts and help for the power wheel
L	Library	Maps and books on your area's geology
M	Blacksmith or engineer	Wheel shafts, etc; kiln frame; fire bars
N	Old town gas works	Kiln bricks; iron oxide
O	Road works and council yard	Clay; rock salt for salt glaze firings; stone dust
P	Local potter	Help and information—also, of course, pots.
R	Church	I have found the local vicar an invaluable source of information
S	Carpentry and joinery workshop	Wood and help for wheel making; offcuts to burn for wood ash; saw dust for brick making
T	Burnt barn or haystack	Lots of wood or straw ash
U	Garage	Waste sump oil. Some garages will do engineering work for kilns and wheels

Ash substitute

When a reliable wood or straw ash is not available the two following mixtures can be used as a synthetic ash. The mixes supply all of the major materials that are found in ashes, but they may lack some of the subtle properties that only genuine ashes can give.

The idea of an ash substitute may seem somewhat bizarre to the purist. Out of curiosity I rewrote all of my ash glaze recipes with these mixes. The resulting fired glazes were close to the originals, and two were much better, and have also proved to give more consistent results.

Mixed wood ash substitute		*Straw ash substitute*	
Potash feldspar	10%	Cornwall stone	30
Whiting	60	Whiting	5
Talc	5	Quartz	65
Bone ash	5		
Ball clay	15		
Quartz	5		

Granite and basalt

A source of finely crushed granite or basalt can be the basis of a whole range of a stoneware and porcelain glazes. This may not be easy to find, but it is worth persevering. Look for a quarry or monumental mason's where granite material is being cut. Cutting produces a very fine dust which is ideal for glaze-making.

The granite dust I obtain has a certain amount of iron in it. Fired to 1250°C, without additions it melts to a mid-brown glaze, rather like chocolate sauce. Because granite has a slightly lower melting temperature than potash feldspar when used in its place my glazes are more fluid, and of course the iron content colours them.

Basalt also contains a large amount of iron. It will melt to an acceptable glaze at about 1250°C, but more attractive glazes will result when it is line blended with other materials.

Granite and other mineral dusts are used in some grades of house paints. I know a potter who lives within a few miles of a paint factory who regularly obtains granite dust from the factory manager. This he uses as the main ingredient for most of his stoneware glazes.

Granite, basalt and many other rocks are ideal stoneware glaze materials.

48

A Dartmoor granite quarry. Like many small quarries, this is a complete industry – the stone is cut and made into head-stones, shop fronts, facing stones etc.

The cutting saw which is cooled by water produces a fine granite slurry, which dries to a fine powder.

The rocks that are of greatest value for glaze making are those that contain a substantial amount of fluxes. An analysis of my local Dartmoor granite shows that it is comprised of roughly equal parts of potash feldspar, soda feldspar and quartz. Its potential as a glaze material is clear, as potash and soda feldspar both contain potassium and sodium. Likewise basalt is rich in the fluxes potassium, sodium, calcium and magnesium. Other useful glaze minerals in my area of England are igneous rock, bone ash and limestone.

Often the finest pulverised rock that a quarry crushing machine will make is granular, and thus still too coarse for glaze-making. Should you have available a reliable supply of such rock you may consider making a ball-mill to grind the granules to a fine powder. If you study the expensive commercially made ball mills you will see how simple it is to make such a machine. All of the parts are readily available including second-hand electric motors with a small gearbox. The only relatively expensive component is the one or two gallon porcelain ball mill, which you may have to buy new from a pottery supplier.

Iron

In sand-pits I have found hematite (iron) that can easily be crushed to a fine powder, usually purple or purple-red in colour. In the old coal gas works red iron oxide was used in the gas purification process. On the sites of these now disused works large piles of this material can often be found.

The water that flows into the well at my pottery is contaminated with yellow ochre which is a mixture of iron and clay. This ochre settles to the bottom in the form of a very fine yellow sludge, which can be removed when the well is drained for cleaning. Similar material can be found in small streams or dykes in some areas.

Iron rust performs a similar function to iron spangles in a glaze, giving speckles, and the substance can be obtained by scraping any rusting iron or steel. An old rusting corrugated iron roof can yield several pounds of glaze materials if a plastic sheet is placed under it and the iron is given a few sharp blows to remove the loose iron rust. My expensive steel kiln chimney keeps me constantly supplied with iron rust.

Clays as a glaze material

Almost any type of clay can be used as a glaze material.

Although china clays and white ball clays do contain small amounts of fluxes and iron, they only have a small influence in the melt of any glaze for which they form part of the recipe, and the main reason for adding china or ball clay to a recipe is to give the glaze alumina and silica. The plasticity of ball clays and other plastic clays is essential for most once-fired glazes. China clay or coarse fireclay does not have enough plasticity to allow the glaze to shrink as it dries, which means it cannot be used in raw glazing (see Chapter 2 on raw glazing).

Alluvial clays, red firing earthenware clay, or the low firing clays that are to be found in the garden, river bank or building site, usually contribute larger amounts of fluxes and iron than those mentioned above. The iron will colour any resulting glaze. Back in geological history these clays were washed down rivers and settled in ancient estuaries or seas, and during this process they were contaminated with useful glaze fluxes and large amounts of iron. The local brickyard clay and the Burns Red clays contain such large amounts of calcium, other fluxes and iron that they will melt to a glaze at about 1250°C without any additions. Line blended with other materials a whole range of handsome glazes can be obtained with these clays. When line blended with potash feldspar, for example, soft variegated green or brown glazes are produced, depending upon whether the pots are fired under reduction or oxidising conditions.

A contaminated clay, such as brickyard clay, has a complex chemical structure. Not only are alumina and silica present, but also large amounts of lime, magnesium, iron and many trace elements. In the firing melt all of these react upon each other producing a very complicated glaze melt, so that simple stoneware and porcelain recipes such as mixes of clay and ash produce subtle and interesting glazes. You will also find it rewarding to line blend contaminated clays with talc, feldspar, and petalite when firing stoneware and porcelain; lead and borax materials for earthenware glazes.

Albany slip is a contaminated alluvial clay

Clay from a river bank. As it is contaminated with large amounts of iron and calcium, this clay cannot be used for pot making, but it makes an ideal slip or glaze material.

containing large amounts of the fluxes potassium, calcium and magnesium, together with iron and the clay minerals alumina and silica. It is mined from various pits scattered throughout the Hudson River Valley from Albany to Catskill, New York. It is the ideal glaze material as it will glaze raw, and without any additions will make a dark shiny glaze at 1170°C, a bright dark brown glaze at 1200°C to 1250°C and an ochre brown glaze at 1280°C. It is also said that it never crazes or shivers. With additions of other glaze materials Albany slip provides an endless source of iron bearing glazes (see section on line blend suggestions, pp. 22–24).

In his book *Oriental Glazes*, Nigel Wood gives a recipe that simulates Albany slip. This is useful if you would like to try a recipe that contains this material, but as it is a complex recipe and there are plenty of good local clays available I do not think it would make a good starting point for new tests.

As it comes out of the ground clay will contain the

Salt glazed teapot, jug and tea bowls made by Michelle Doherty. Michelle enhances the subtle quality of salt glazing by wood firing her pots and using a wide range of slips.

odd stone, root, etc., as well as moisture. To prepare it as a glaze material it has to be dried, crushed and then sieved through a 40 mesh sieve. A simple way of drying the clay is to lay it on a plastic sheet in the sun; even in the workshop it will soon dry. It can then be put into a strong plastic sack and pulverised to a powder by beating the sack with a mallet. The clay is now ready for sieving. Remember all dust is potentially hazardous, so take precautions by covering the top of the sieve and wearing a dust-mask.

Clays are one of the most rewarding of all glaze materials and usually the easiest to find, as they lie under most top soils. Even the city dweller can find excellent materials on building sites and road works. A kind word and the present of the odd pot can work wonders with a site foreman.

Local materials have the great advantage of costing very little, or nothing, but I feel the main reason for searching them out is for the quality and originality they can give to a glaze. I have just related my experience of local materials, but in different parts of every country there will be useful glaze ingredients available to the inquiring potter.

Clays for pot making

Throughout the countryside good pot making, plastic earthenware clays can be found. When dug they can be many colours: black, orange-red to brown, yellow or even a dirty yellow-green, but they nearly all fire to terracotta red. Occasionally a pocket of white firing, iron-free earthenware clay can be found.

The contaminated earthenware clays will not withstand stoneware temperatures, and unfortunately, purer clay suitable for making stoneware pots is less widely distributed. There are ideal plastic stoneware clays that have all of the qualities that the potter desires, but these are very rare. Plastic fireclays or ballclays are more easily found but they do not have the ideal fired qualities desired by most craft potters. These clays are used as the basis for blended stoneware clay bodies' of various clays, sand, feldspar and quartz (see Chapter 2, pp. 71–3).

As you will need a much larger quantity of clay for pot making than required for glazes, you must consider whether the rewards of local potting clay are great enough to compensate for the hard work of digging and preparing it. A superb seam of plastic and beautiful firing clay is worth the blisters and backache, but if your local clay is no better than average maybe your time would be better spent potting!

As far as I know China is the only place where porcelain clay can be found. As the Chinese do not as yet export petuntse, other porcelain potters have to derive their clay from a mix from china clay, feldspar, quartz, ballclay and bentonite clay.

Very few clays are clean enough to be potted as dug; they usually contain roots, stones, and grit. Most clays need to be watered down to a slip and sieved through a 20 to 40 mesh sieve to remove the debris, and are then brought back to throwing consistency by drying out on large plaster bats or in thick biscuited bowls. Should you wish to prepare large quantities of clay a drying pan can be constructed. This is a trough made of absorbent house bricks, made so that air can circulate beneath the bricks to assist drying. In warmer and drier climates than Great Britain the clay can be dried on old sheets laid on the bare earth.

Safety in the pottery

Unless simple precautions are taken the pottery workshop can be a hazardous place.

Obvious dangers arise when kilns, wheels, pugmills, etc., are misused. The hidden dangers come from pottery materials. The two main concerns are the toxic nature of certain finely ground materials, which can easily be breathed in while preparing glazes, and the toxic metal release from certain fired glazes. The glaze surface may be attacked by acids present in foodstuffs, and so be contaminated.

The following materials should be regarded as potentially hazardous:

Antimony oxide
Barium carbonate
Borax
Chromium oxide
Copper oxide
Copper carbonate
Flint
Galena (lead sulphide)
Lead carbonate (white lead)

Litharge (yellow lead)
Manganese carbonate
Manganese dioxide
Nickel oxide
Quartz
Red lead
Vanadium pentoxide

Precautions against being poisoned by toxic materials in the pottery

1 It is important that the pottery is swept clean regularly. A sweeping compound or wet sawdust should be applied to the floor before sweeping. As some disturbance will inevitably be created and minute particles will become airborne it should be done at the end of the day, when work has finished.
2 Do not eat or smoke in the workshop.
3 If possible prepare materials by wet processes, to avoid creating dust. Any dry preparation of finely-ground materials is best done out of doors, while wearing a face mask.

Precautions against metal release from fired glazes

1 Glazes that contain lead compound or antimony, and cadmium should be tested for metal release if there is even the remotest possibility of food or drink being used in a pot that has any of these materials in its glaze. Below are the addresses of testing laboratories, which test glazes for metal release:
    Bio-Technics Labs, Inc., 1133 Crenshaw Blvd., Los Angeles, CA 90019   Coors Spectro-Chemical Lab, Box 5865, Denver, CO 80217   Pittsburgh Testing Lab, 850 Poplar St., Pittsburgh, PA 15220.
2 Do not use copper in any domestic ware lead glazes, as it can make an otherwise safe glaze toxic.
3 See page 24 for further notes on earthenware glazes.

2 Raw glazing

Raw glazing

The direct method of once-fired ware (also called raw glazing) has been practised by craft potters throughout history. I feel that biscuit firing adds nothing to the liveliness and freshness of the craft pottery process.

Until the industrialisation of pottery in the nineteenth century most potters raw glazed and once-fired their ware. In industry one of the main reasons for introducing biscuiting was that it enabled the ware to be stored in a fixed condition prior to being glazed. Not having to glaze and finish 'green' pots also enabled the industrial potter to employ less skilled labour.

Many of today's craft potters biscuit fire their pots, because they learnt their skills initially at an art school or college, where teaching was biassed towards industry. Biscuiting has been perpetuated as knowledge has passed from one generation to the next, for once a potter has devised a viable working method it can be hard to give that up to learn a new and unknown set of skills.

When I started potting, once-firing pots seemed to me to be a logical, natural process. I became a potter because of my interest and sympathy with the traditional country potter, and the country potter through the centuries made his pots simply, raw glazed and once-fired them.

Having had some experience of packing, firing and unpacking biscuit kilns, then having to glaze large amounts of unsympathetic hard, brittle biscuit pots, I came to the conclusion that raw glazing would not only save me fuel and time, but, much more important, would give me a more enjoyable way of making pots.

As there is no biscuit firing to interrupt the making process, the making, glazing and firing of pots is

Lead amber glazed butter dish by Suzi Cree. This has been decorated by combing through a white slip; a green copper pigment has been used on the exterior of the pot only. In her words: 'I think I started raw glazing for the obvious reasons of saving fuel and time. But I found that the sensitivity I had developed through working with creamy slip on leather-hard clay naturally extended to using slip-glazes. Raw glazing gives the making process a rhythmic fluency, which I hope is reflected in my finished pots.'

uninterrupted. This encourages a natural rhythm in the workshop, which I hope is reflected in the finished ware.

Choice of method

There are two basic methods of raw glazing pots: glazing when the pots are bone dry with non-plastic glazes (sometimes with additions of various gums) or glazing when leather hard. Dry glazing can be very successful with the more generously potted wares, but less so for finer pots. The main problems encountered are cracking, distortion and the dissolving of fine edges, lips, etc.

If your pots have simple shapes and are fairly thickly potted try the dry glaze method—glazes with little or no plastic clay in them such as you may have derived for biscuit ware will often work well on bone dry clay. The technique is similar to that of glazing biscuit ware. For a potter making robust plant pots, heavy ovenware or similar pots dry glazing could be ideal.

Having tried dry glazing I found it too precarious for my range of domestic stoneware, which is too thinly potted for this technique. So I began to use the leather hard method, as this does not force me to make over-robust pots in order to withstand the glazing process. The ware is glazed when leather-hard with glazes that contain plastic clay (not china or coarse fireclay). When drying the clay content allows the glaze to shrink at the same rate as the pot. Without clay in the glaze it would flake off the pot.

Any recipe that contains 20% or more of plastic clay will raw glaze successfully. The particle size of coarse fireclay and china clay is too large to contribute plasticity to a glaze. These clays can be used along with plastic clays in a raw glaze if they are required to contribute some other quality, such as colour or texture.

When glazing leather-hard pots the glaze can be applied as thickly or as thinly as desired, whereas glazing bone dry pots invariably means glazing thinly.

Glazing leather-hard is part of the making process and is done while the original concept of the work is fresh, rather than as an afterthought. When glazing dry on biscuited pots the glaze is applied some days or even weeks after the pots have been completed, and this is often done as a necessary chore, the initial enthusiasm for the pots having waned.

To illustrate why I am an enthusiastic leather-hard glazer I recount here a typical day in my workshop:

9.05 a.m.	Look around the shelves and plan the day's work.
9.10 a.m.	Glaze four boards of jugs and five boards of mugs. All these have been handled the previous day.
11.00 a.m.	Coffee. Turn six large bowls and glaze them.
12 noon	Handle two boards of one pint lidded soup bowls. These will be glazed some time tomorrow.
1 p.m.	Lunch
2 p.m.	Glaze a dozen large casseroles that are now overall leather-hard. These were turned and handled yesterday.
3 p.m.	Coffee. Prepare clay and throw teapot bodies.
5 p.m. to 6.30 p.m.	End of work day. Tea-time.

Large salt glazed jar, 41 cm high, made by the Dutch potter Joop Crompuoets. The interior was raw glazed when the pot was bone-dry. Joop's robust potting style is ideal for bone-dry raw glazing.

No two days are the same. Every day brings a varied and different range of tasks.

A few potters who work in hotter and drier climates than England dismiss this method of glazing, as they fear that their pots will dry out before they are able to catch them at the leather-hard stage. I have found that even during the hottest and driest days that summer can bring boards of pots covered with thin plastic sheeting will remain leather-hard for at least ten days. If there is time enough when the pots are leather-hard to turn them and put on handles, spouts, lugs, etc., there must be time to glaze them. In short, if you can apply slips to your pots, you will be able to raw glaze your ware.

All of the glaze recipes in the 'base glazes' section of this book (pp. 27–30) as well as being good biscuit ware glazes are ideal for leather-hard raw glazing because of their high clay content.

Glaze application

When your methods have been established raw glazing earthenware and stoneware clays should pose no problems. Generally pots can be glazed in any condition from soft leather-hard to almost dry. Raw glazing porcelain, however, requires quite a degree of skill, especially if one is potting the porcelain very finely to achieve translucency; here the glaze tends to saturate the very thin pot and cause it to collapse. Usually translucency in porcelain is only striven for in the walls and the rims as these are areas of the pot that bear little stress. Therefore a collapse is unlikely if the base or foot of the pot are potted rather more substantially.

I find no problems when glazing porcelain as I am not striving for translucency, though often my pots are slightly translucent on their rims or on the upper part of their body. I make porcelain for its glaze clarity and beauty. No other glazes have the 'depth' of porcelain glazes. Some give you the impression that you are looking into infinity.

If you wish to make 'eggshell' thin porcelain pots raw glazing may not be practical and the inconvenience of biscuiting has to be considered. Colin Pearson who raw glazes a wide range of stoneware domestic and individual pots does biscuit his thin small porcelain individual pieces, though he does raw glaze some of his larger porcelain pieces where translucency is not of paramount importance.

Raw glazing pots that are to be salt-glazed is a very simple process, as usually the ware only requires glazing on the inside. Any of the non-matt 1230°C to 1300°C base glazes on pp. 28–9 are ideal for this purpose.

Thickness of raw glazes

When glaze is applied to a raw unbiscuited pot it does not suck the glaze water into itself like a biscuited pot; the glazed raw pot has to dry naturally. As less water is taken into the pot raw glazes have to be thicker than biscuit glazes. If you think of the consistency of an average biscuit glaze as milk, a raw glaze is cream in comparison.

Glaze materials such as nepheline syenite and some clays contain soluble soda salts which can deflocculate the glaze. The soda causes the glaze to be extremely runny so that when it is applied to a pot it does not bind with the clay but runs off. Soluble soda can easily be neutralized by adding a small amount of acetic acid or vinegar to the glaze mix, which often has a dramatic effect. What was formerly a thin runny glaze will fizz and bubble and after a few minutes will be so thick that more water has to be added to bring it to the correct consistency. Approximately $\frac{1}{4}$ pt of acetic acid or vinegar added to 2 gallons of glaze should be sufficient. Sometimes after a few weeks the soluble soda will start deflocculating the glaze once more, so the treatment will have to be repeated.

Raw glazing simple ware

The average potter who biscuit fires his pots gains over a period of years a repertoire of skills in the glazing of biscuit ware. Although most of the skills used in biscuit glazing are relevant to glazing unfired pots, there are some subtle differences, and a slightly new technique is required. Even established potters who have been attracted to raw glazing and once firing have been discouraged because their initial attempts did not yield the results they had hoped for. This is why I recommend that your first firing of raw glazed pots should be restricted to a few simple items, such as small bowls, beakers or egg cups. These should be included in a normal glaze firing of biscuited pots. By starting this way a gradual understanding is acquired and as confidence grows, larger and more complicated pots can be glazed and included in the firings. Over a period of five or six firings à novice raw glazer can be weaned onto raw glazing all of their ware without any major mishaps or loss of quality in the finished product.

Bowls, mugs, cups and saucers, beakers, bottles, oven dishes, goblets, casseroles, store jars, porringers, candlesticks: the items listed here can all be glazed by the following technique. As I have previously explained a raw glaze is applied much thicker than an equivalent biscuit glaze as raw pots do not suck water out of the glaze like biscuited pots.

Simple domestic ware made by the author, and glazed by the methods demonstrated overleaf.

1 The thrown one pint jug. On this particular jug I have brushed the slip, which subtly alters the colour of the fired glaze.

2 Unglazed leatherhard pots. The handles have been put on. The whole pot is allowed to dry to a uniform leather hardness before glazing.

4 Pouring out the glaze.

5 Wiping glaze off the exterior of the pot.

7 Glazing exterior of the pot. This can be done by either dipping, pouring or spraying.

8 Glazed pots drying; they are left to become bone dry before firing.

3 Glazing the interior of the jug.

6 Pots left to dry back to leatherhard.

9 The finished fired jug. This particular glaze is a version of base glaze 1.

Pour a quantity of glaze into the leather-hard pot and rinse round to coat the inside. Wipe off any glaze that adheres to the outside or rim of the pot with a clean damp sponge, removing the glaze with one precise clean wipe. If one is over-fussy the clay can look tired, sandy and overworked, and this applies especially to any clay surfaces that are to remain unglazed. Glaze left on the outside or rim of the pot may cause flaking off when the exterior is glazed. Replace the pot on its board and allow it to dry back to leather-hard. The pot is then ready to have the outside glazed, which can be done by either dipping, pouring or spraying. Some potters glaze the outside of their pots immediately after glazing the inside, before the pot has had time to become saturated by the interior glaze. I prefer to glaze my pots in two separate operations as there is some danger of the pot distorting if it becomes too wet with glaze.

Earthenware, which generally is potted a little thicker than stoneware or porcelain, is more easily glazed in one operation.

Porcelain should always be glazed in two operations but dividing the glazing operation into two separate stages does not involve an undue amount of extra time. The glaze is best applied when the pot is dry leather-hard.

In my workshop in the summertime pots that have been glazed inside during the morning have dried back to leather-hard by the afternoon and are ready to have the outsides glazed. In the wintertime the cycle takes twenty-four hours. A harmonious working rhythm is soon established.

It perplexes me that some potters dismiss raw glazing, but competently use slips on their pots. The application technique is almost identical and raw glazing should therefore hold no fears.

63

Glazing tea pots and coffee pots

Tea pots, coffee pots, and other pots with spouts can be glazed when completed by the same method used for the simpler pots. Alternatively, I have found the following method is easier and quicker when making quantities of this type of pot.

Thrown body of the pot.

Waxing the gallery of the leatherhard pot. Any turning of leatherhard pot or its lid is done before waxing.

Glazing the interior of the body of the pot. The body of the pot is allowed to dry back to leatherhard.

First make the body and lid of the pot. Allow the pot to dry to leather-hard, and then turn the foot of the pot if required. Turn the lid and make a knob for it and wax the pot where necessary. The inside of the body and the lid are glazed when leather-hard. When the pot has dried back to leather-hard cut the strainer holes and join the spout and handle (or lugs for a cane

The strainer for the spout is cut and the spout and handle are added to the pot. The whole pot is allowed to dry back to a uniform leatherhardness before glazing.

Glazing the exterior of the pot. This can be done by either dipping, pouring or spraying.

Glazed pots drying. These are left to dry to bone dry before firing.

The finished fired teapot. The glaze is a version of glaze 4 (see page 29).

handle) to the body. If the handle is pulled on the pot and/or the spout is applied wet directly from the wheel these will have to be allowed to dry to the same uniform leather-hardness of the whole pot before glazing the exterior. As with any other pot this can be done by spraying, pouring or dipping. When dipping or pouring the glaze onto the exterior of the tea-pot the glaze never runs up the entire length of the inside of

Stoneware teapot made by Andrew and Joanna Young. The Youngs raw glaze and once-fire their ware.

the spout, so the strainer never becomes blocked with glaze.

Written down it sounds complicated, but in practice I have found this is a quick and troublefree method, and demonstrates one of the joys of raw glazing, that the making and glazing are completely integrated.

Problem pots

Usually a potter has within his repertoire one or two items that will initially present seemingly insoluble problems for raw glazing, but I have not found a pot that could not be glazed raw, if the making and glazing techniques are taken back to first principles and completely rethought. For example, my cider and wine jars (see photograph, page 30) of a capacity of one to five gallons used to present me with problems, until I changed my glazing method. I used to glaze the interior and exterior of the jar before cutting and inserting the bung-hole (which accepts the wooden tap). Now I complete the jar with the bung-hole inserted in the base. The bung-hole is sealed by gluing a small piece of paper over it with carpet glue. This allows the interior of the jar to be glazed without glaze pouring out of the bung-hole, and when the jar has dried back

Figure 3 Circled are parts of the pot that may distort or crack when raw glazed. Slightly thicker potting at these points will correct this.

to leather-hard and the exterior is glazed it stops glaze rushing up the neck of the jar, because the sealed bung-hole creates an airlock. The paper is easily peeled off after the pot has been glazed.

I encountered problems when glazing big turned plates. About a third of them did not survive the glazing process; the thickly glazed centre of the plate slumped and cracked. The thinly trimmed plate became over-saturated and was not strong enough to support a thick application of glaze. I overcame this by glazing the plate before trimming its foot. I now trim the plate with its rim resting on a soft ring of clay so the glazed plate is not marked.

Before I raw glazed all of my ware I occasionally lost some pots through squatting or distortion during the firing. This usually happened because they had been trimmed too thinly. When raw glazing any uneven throwing or thin-trimming becomes apparent as a badly made raw pot will not stand up to the wet glaze. Initially it can be very frustrating to have the odd pot collapse after having spent time making and glazing it, but soon one ends up making a better finished product, with the clay properly distributed through the pots.

I have never encountered any problems of 'glaze fit', such as the glaze flaking off rims or knobs, because all of my glazes have a high clay content. Should you occasionally encounter this problem but not wish to alter the glaze recipe, a drop of methyl cellulose glaze hardener in the glaze can work wonders.

Certain glazes may also crawl because of excessive body shrinkage, a problem which can be cured if the body shrinkage is cut down to an acceptable amount. I have never encountered crawling due to the glaze having been applied over dirt or grease. This seems to be a problem exclusive to biscuit ware.

Decorating and double glaze application

The decorating techniques used on biscuit ware can be used with equal success on raw pots. Over and under glaze painting, paper and wax resist, use of slip, and so on, present no particular problems. It is far easier to under-glaze decorate raw pots than biscuit ware, as the brush does not cling to the clay as it does to absorbent biscuit.

What can excite the newcomer to glazing raw is that several new decorative techniques are available. This is because the glaze does not dry on the pot immediately, but remains wet and fluid for a while, affording many more decorative possibilities. Also, as the glaze is applied over a leather-hard pot rather than a hard biscuited one, sgraffito can be used in a very bold manner through the glaze into the clay.

While the glaze remains wet there is time for two or more glazes to be slip-trailed on to a pot. The pot can then be agitated to make the glazes flow and produce a marbled effect.

Another wet glaze method that is a little unpredictable but can be very pleasing is applying a second glaze over the first while it is still wet. This technique requires deft and quick handling and an intimate knowledge of what glazes are compatible. A few small tests will indicate the best combinations.

The decorative technique I particularly like is combing or brushing the wet glaze just after it has been applied. A fairly stiff brush is used in a non-fussy direct manner to wipe away an area of glaze revealing the clay beneath. The brush also pushes the glaze aside giving a thicker line of glaze next to the brush mark.

Three small store jars made by the author, variously glazed and decorated by wiping away the glaze with a stiff brush while it is still wet.

An extension of this technique is to comb or brush a decorative motif through the glaze and apply a second glaze later when the pot has dried back to leather-hard. This gives areas where only the second glaze is present, contrasting with the double glazed area. In stoneware and porcelain I use this technique with dry ash yellow and orange and red glazes, over which I apply shiny or semi-glossy transparent glazes. By this method a range of high fired glaze colours can be obtained that are a little different from the norm. For example, the cider jar on page 30 was first glazed in a yellow matt ash/clay glaze and later a glossy semi-transparent iron red glaze was applied. The resulting fired glaze is a slightly glossy ochre-yellow where both thicknesses of glaze are present, a red line of the same texture being revealed where the under glaze has been brushed away.

I also use this method of double glazing without any combing or brushing simply to achieve the unique glaze colours that this technique creates. Considerable variations of colour and texture can be achieved by varying the thicknesses of the two glazes. For example, with the ash yellow and shiny red combination, the thicker the yellow and thinner the red, the brighter is the resulting yellow glaze. With a thin ash yellow and a thick red application, the result is a red glaze which breaks to ochre on the rim and belly of the pot where the glaze thins.

When experimenting with double glazing remember that any shiny glaze over any matt glaze is likely to produce interesting results. A matt glaze over a shiny glaze will usually produce a bubbly or broken surface. Sometimes this can be attractive if used on the exterior of a pot or on non-functional ware. Shiny glazes used on top of one another will produce good results, but they tend not to produce such distinctive glazes.

Adjusting glazes

Non-raw glaze recipes that contain 15% or more of china clay will normally work very well raw if the china clay is substituted with white ball clay, plus 3% bentonite. If the fired result is a little shinier or matter than the original this can usually be adjusted by adding a little more ball clay or quartz (up to 10% of each) to the recipe.

Bentonite, an extremely plastic clay, is often added to raw glazes when the clay content of a recipe is slightly low. I have found that 5% of bentonite is the maximum amount required. Larger amounts will not increase the plasticity of the glaze.

When preparing a glaze containing bentonite, the rules of normal safe glaze making procedure have to be broken as this material is not easily dispersed throughout a glaze. If the glaze materials are added to water the bentonite will congeal in a sticky lump. Therefore the bentonite and other materials should first be mixed thoroughly together when dry. (See safety notes on preparation of dry materials, page 55)

Waxing

Wiping the glaze from the raw clay is laborious and can leave an unpleasant surface. On such areas rather than wipe away, I use wax , carpet glue or rubber cement. This does not reject the glaze as candle wax does, but easily peels away when the glaze has dried, leaving a good clean edge. Carpet glue is fairly expensive, but I have come to prefer it as it is simple and easy to use. Brushes should be washed out in white spirit directly after use.

Wax is just as easy as carpet glue to apply and does have the advantage of being relatively inexpensive. Moreover, it can be used in its own right as a decorative technique. In my experience, though, hot wax containers have the nasty habit of bursting into flames if left unattended, so treat them with due respect; they are a potential fire-hazard.

Clay bodies—earthenware, stoneware and porcelain

Earthenware, stoneware and porcelain clays can all be successfully raw glazed. The only problem I have encountered is edge peeling of the glaze when the pot dries on some stoneware clay bodies, where the clay mixtures concerned have all been studio potters' personal recipes devised for biscuit firing. These recipes have had large amounts of high shrinkage ball clays in them; on drying the glaze was unable to shrink as much as the pots, causing the glaze to peel off the edges. Such clay bodies are easily adjusted by adding 10% to 20% of china clay. This will alter the shrinkage characteristics of the body to ensure a good glaze fit. If the china clay is added to the body as a slip the plasticity and consequently the throwing qualities of the clay body will not suffer. I have found that adding china clay to a stoneware clay will often improve its fired colour.

Below are three very plastic stoneware throwing recipes based on ball clays that are suitable for oxidising, reduction and salt-glazed firings.

1	Ball clay	56 lb
	Fireclay (sieved through a 30 mesh sieve)	30 lb
	Red earthenware clay	12 lb
	Quartz	5 lb
2	Ball clay	56 lb
	Fireclay (sieved through a 30 mesh sieve)	36 lb
	Red iron oxide	$0-1\frac{1}{2}$ lb

Without the iron oxide this mix makes a good salt-glaze body. For oxidized and reduced stoneware the colour will vary from cream or light-grey to dark-red or brown depending upon how much iron is introduced into the mix.

Theoretically, adding iron oxide to colour a reduction stoneware clay body can be a dangerous practice as it can cause the fired pots to shatter, but I have found this recipe to be wholly reliable. The other common method of colouring a stoneware body is to add red earthenware clay to the mix, but this too can cause problems as red earthenware clays often contain calcium, large amounts of carbon and other impurities. These can introduce such difficulties as bloating (blistering of the clay) and warping in the firing; the carbon escaping at high temperatures can also cause the glaze surface to blister. These problems are discussed on pp. 73–5.

3	English china clays, HYPLAS 71 ball clay	75 lb
	Ball clay	24 lb
	Cornwall stone	1 lb

This clay body recipe is used by many British potters, because of its fired strength and its plasticity without undue shrinkage. It fires well to an off-white colour and if wood fired it toasts to a light orange colour.

I mix my own clay. I am ideally situated living in Devon, and my pottery is within a few miles of numerous clay pits mining some of the best clays in England. Buying various clays from them and mixing them myself gives me a clay with all the properties I desire: fired strength, colour, texture and price.

Small amounts of clay can be mixed in a large bin. I mix in an old baker's doughmixer, which I found in an old village bakery. It cost me a coffee pot!

Firing raw glazed pots

Firing pots that you have raw glazed is remarkably easy if the few precautions I list below are observed.

There are two critical times when firing raw pots: when the kiln is at a temperature of between 50°C and 100°C, and between the temperatures of 900°C and 1000°C. If care is taken at these times during the firing cycle, then firing raw pots is a very simple exercise.

In my own kiln, which is a 100 cubic ft down-draught oil-fired kiln, the pots are packed as closely as possible. I don't worry if the pots are damp or if they are slightly touching one another, as they will contract and shrink away from each other during firing.

After closing and sealing the door of the kiln I place a small propane gas torch in the mouth of the fire box. This is left burning for approximately twelve hours. The temperature in the kiln chamber is held at just below 100°C. This preheating thoroughly dries out the pots, eliminating any danger of breakages due to water vapour escaping too rapidly. A similar procedure should be adopted when once-firing any type of kiln. In an electric kiln the power control should be set on the lowest setting, and the top spy hole left open. This should keep the kiln at below 100°C to allow the pots to become thoroughly dry. In small kilns I have found a preheating time of two to three hours is more than adequate.

After preheating my kiln I ignite the oil burners. The burners are gradually turned up until after approximately seven hours the chamber has reached a temperature of 950°C. At this stage I turn back the burners until they are giving a short, very bright flame. They remain at this setting for 1 hour, and the temperature is held at below 1000°C, which enables the carbon present in the clay and glazes to be burnt out.

Raw glazed pots ready for firing.

Without the 'cleaning' burn these impurities would remain trapped in the pots as the clay and glazes melt and seal their surfaces, possibly causing such problems as blistering, bloating and pinholing.

When firing earthenware pots this particular burn should be held at just below 900°C because earthenware glazes start to melt at a lower temperature than stoneware glazes.

When firing an electric kiln it is possible to set the power control at a point where the temperature remains steady at between 900°C and 1000°C. If this is maintained for one hour, the cleaning burn will have been adequately accomplished.

Following the cleaning burn I reduce fire my kiln for up to seven hours until my maximum temperature of 1250°C has been reached. Reduction is obtained by half closing the damper, reducing the secondary air holes by half and slightly increasing the fuel to the burners. After reduction I reoxidize the chamber for fifteen minutes, which has the effect of toasting the clay body,

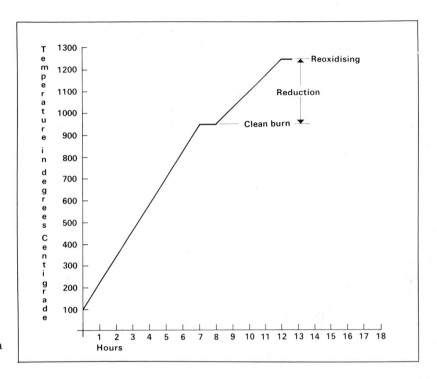

Figure 4 The graph shows the typical firing cycle of my large oil kiln. When firing big pots or any thick sculptural piece, I extend the firing by two or three hours between 100° and 700°C as a precaution.

making it much more red and it also slightly increases the gloss on the glaze surface.

For an earthenware firing after the cleaning burn the kiln should be turned up until the maximum temperature has been reached (usually between 1040°C and 1180°C). Most earthenware potters like to 'soak' their glazes for a short while at this maximum temperature.

As pyrometers are expensive and often unreliable, I use pyrometric cones to establish the kiln temperature. I use three cones. The first bends at 940°C for the clean burn, the second at 1230°C which indicates that the maximum firing temperature has almost been reached and the third at 1250°C for the maximum temperature. Cones are invaluable as they show the amount of 'heat work' done rather than the actual chamber temperature.

After firing my kiln it is sealed and allowed to cool. Initially there is a fast drop in temperature, but subsequently the cooling rate slows. It is some eighteen hours before the kiln can be opened.

Whether you are firing your pots by electricity, gas, oil, coal or wood if you can devise a similar firing procedure, once-firing raw pots should present very few problems.

Unglazed ware

Unglazed earthenware is a very enjoyable, but neglected area of craft pottery. There is a growing interest in plant pots of all sizes, hanging bowls, patio pots, and so on. Simple garden pots decorated boldly by combing, adding colouring oxides and applied clay can be great fun to make and a joy to use.

In almost every part of the country there is suitable clay to be found for making earthenware pots. If your garden does not yield a suitable clay, good red firing plastic clay can always be found at a brick works, and it is surprising how many current and disused clay pits can be found. After removing the odd stone or so, the clay can generally be used as dug.

Unglazed earthenware burnished dish 8 × 9 inches, with incised decoration by Siddig El'Nigoumi.

Above: unglazed earthenware pot
from Kenya.
Below: yellow-coated pink
earthenware flagon painted red
and purple from Faras; Nubian,
1st or 2nd century AD (*Ashmolean
Museum*).

3 Simple kiln building

You may have guessed that I am a little prejudiced against electric kilns. I admit that for both earthenware and stoneware oxidised firings they are efficient, but they do lack romance. A kiln that has flames crackling and roaring through evokes so much more enthusiasm. When a fuel is actually being burned the atmosphere in the kiln chamber can easily be controlled, but although tortuous experiments have been made to produce a good reducing atmosphere in electric kilns, they are only really suitable for oxidised firings. An oil, gas or wood burning kiln can produce with ease an atmosphere in the kiln chamber ranging from that of clean oxidisation to smoky reduction, depending on your requirements.

It is a great shame that our schools and evening classes are so hidebound by safety regulations and insist upon expensive modern kiln technology. Education authorities equip their potteries with expensive kilns which have programmed firing controls, over-elaborate safety devices, and other costly electronic gadgets. Pots are put into these magic boxes and a few hours later the finished pot is returned to its owner. How much more could have been learned if the students had made their own simple kiln and fired it themselves.

The alternative to the expensive magic box is to build yourself a small kiln from readily available materials. The first two designs have been used many times and have produced efficient kilns that fire quickly and easily; they are made of traditional fire brick. Minimal brick laying skills are required for making these kilns—little more than the ability to put one brick on top of another. With the relatively expensive new materials ceramic fibre, blanket, board and blocks, you can build super-efficient light kilns. My

A simple kiln built by the students of Medway College of Design – see kiln design 1

78

third basic design relies on these new materials, but with an eye to cost and simplicity of construction.

Choice of kiln

I have tried to present the advantages and disadvantages of the various kilns in a logical sequence, to help you plan and build a kiln that is best suited to your particular potting needs.

Decision one—size of kiln

The capacity of the kiln controls the potter's complete working cycle. If your kiln is too small you waste too much time and fuel repeatedly firing small amounts of ware. The larger the kiln the more fuel-efficient it becomes and also, as it takes almost as much time to pack, fire and unpack a small kiln as a large one, it means a larger kiln gives more time for making pots. Because bigger kilns are not fired so often, they will last longer. On the other hand if too large a kiln is built the potter's work cycle can be too long; this can be frustrating as enthusiasm is maintained by a regular flow of new pots and tests. I have found that to test and refine a new glaze or clay body takes from three to six firings and with a big kiln this process could take a year or more. Firing a big kiln can be a traumatic experience as 'all the eggs are in one basket'.

The question is how often will you want to fire your kiln—when you know the answer to this you will know the size of kiln you have to build.

Once you have decided what size of kiln you wish to build, the type of arch it is going to have is as good as decided for you. A small kiln (one to four cubic feet) may have its roof made of one or two kiln shelves. A larger kiln will require a proper arch. The basic types of arch are the catenary arch and the sprung arch.

The catenary arch is a self-supporting structure. The catenary is the inverted shape that a chain makes when it is hung in a loop. This arch has the advantage of not needing ironwork to support it, so it is a relatively simple structure to build.

The sprung arch does not make the complete kiln chamber, as does the catenary arch. It roofs over the vertical walls of the kiln chamber, creating a cubed kiln with an arched roof, which is easy to pack. The main disadvantage of a sprung arch is that it is not self-supporting, and needs a strong steel bracing to hold it. The steel work makes it a complex structure to build. Except where larger kilns are concerned, I feel that the difficulties in construction outweigh the advantages of its having vertical chamber walls. In this book, I am not attempting to deal with kilns of a chamber larger than thirty cubic feet, so if you feel that your potting routine requires a bigger, more complex kiln, I recommend your visiting the local potters and examining their kilns. With further reading (see book list) and good advice, you should be equipped to tackle the building of a big beast.

Decision two—fuel

The main factors determining the fuel you use to fire your kiln with are your personal preference, the cost and its availability.

Wood

Wood is the preferred fuel of many potters as the fly ash from the wood can toast and 'flash' the ware, giving it a richness and warmth unique to wood-fired pots. More than any other type of firing, wood firing is an art that has to be learned by practice. It is also hard work preparing and stoking the timber. With the increasing popularity of wood-burning stoves in some areas offcuts and slabwood from saw mills and timber merchants are becoming expensive, if not scarce. Before deciding upon building a wood firing kiln, ensure that a cheap and plentiful source of good timber is available.

Gas

Firing small kilns with a tank of propane gas and a blow torch burner is simple and convenient, but relatively expensive (see photo on p. 139). When firing domestic ware by propane I have often found that the cost of the firing can be greater than the value of the fired pots. New concepts in kiln design using high insulation materials such as ceramic fibre bricks use propane much more efficiently.

In this book I have discounted other gas fired kilns as they are more complex and can be no longer called 'simple kilns'.

Oil

Even taking into account the dramatic increase in oil prices in the last few years oil is still a viable and convenient kiln fuel. Central heating or gas oil is the most convenient grade of oil, as it flows readily without preheating and has a good heat to price ratio.

Sump oil or garage waste oil does require filtering and preheating to make it flow freely. Although it needs more work to collect and clean it, it has two big advantages. First, it can impart a warm toasted quality similar to that of wood-fired ware. Second, most garage owners are more than happy to find someone to take the messy stuff away and will sell it cheaply or give it to you.

Decision three—type of brick

Kilns for firing low temperature earthenware and raku (up to 1050°C) can be built of cheap new or second-hand house bricks. Above this temperature house bricks start to deform and melt. For higher temperature earthenware, stoneware or porcelain, therefore, expensive firebricks are needed.

There are two basic types of firebrick. 'Hard' firebrick, as its name implies, is dense, solid and hard wearing, but this type of brick has poor insulating qualities. A kiln built of these will use considerably more fuel than one built with soft insulating firebrick (IFB—available from Babcock and Wilcox, P.O. Box 923, Augusta, GA 30903), which is a 'light' porous brick. This is soft and less strong, but for most kiln chambers is thought to be ideal because of its high insulating properties.

For all but salt-glazed kilns the ideal kiln structure would have heavy bricks for the floor and firebox, which is where strength and durability is most needed. In the kiln chamber walls and roof where maximum insulating properties are required IFBs are ideal.

Salt vapour quickly destroys high temperature insulating bricks so kilns for salt glazing should be built of heavy firebricks. Heavy firebricks are attacked by salt vapour, but as they are solid only the 'hot face' is affected and eroded. Because of its open texture the IFB brick is also eaten away from the inside.

As most potters wish to build their kiln as inexpensively as possible it is not always possible to get things absolutely as you might wish. IFB firebricks are up to three times as expensive as heavy firebricks so you have to balance spending more money on purchasing IFBs for your kiln against their fuel saving capacity. You can, however, build a relatively cheap kiln and endure slightly slower firings as the heavies soak up the heat, increasing costs. The softness of IFB bricks makes them easy to cut with a bow saw, or they may be quickly shaped by rubbing on a concrete block. Cutting hard brick is difficult work and has to be done with a hammer and cold chisel.

Both types of brick are made in various qualities. For kiln firings in the 1250°C to 1300°C range, K26 or K28 quality is recommended. This number denotes the temperature the bricks have been fired to in hundreds of degrees Fahrenheit.

By prospecting your own area and looking through the pottery magazines for advertisements good condition second-hand bricks can be obtained. Hard bricks are plentiful and bricks in good condition should cost no more than 10% of the new price. IFBs are a little more scarce as they are more delicate and consequently do not survive over-robust demolition work. A fair price for good second-hand IFBs would be about 20% of the new price.

Old gas works in the past have been a rich source of bricks, but this is drying up. Nowadays the local brickworks is a good source of supply. The linings of brick kilns are frequently renewed and a greater number of the old bricks are in excellent condition. A visit to local commercial potteries will usually prove profitable. Even if you don't come away with any bricks, you will probably get sound information about where they may be found.

Warning! The standard hard brick, $9 \times 4\frac{1}{2} \times 2\frac{1}{2}$, weighs approximately 9 lbs. The two hundred or so needed to build a small kiln will weigh 16 cwt. Several journeys will have to be made in the family car, or more suitable transport will have to be arranged.

Insulating the kiln
To help preserve the heat in the kiln chamber a second skin of bricks should be laid to clad the kiln. You need not use expensive IFBs for this. Common house brick, cinder blocks or your own cinder and clay blocks will suffice. See the section on brick-making, p. 97.

Decision four—kiln site

Ideally a kiln should be sited in the countryside or the more open suburbs. With discretion, kilns can be fired in built-up areas without creating a nuisance; firing a kiln for a few hours every month creates only a very minimal amount of pollution. See section on the art of kiln firing, p. 99.

The ideal kiln shed is a dry, airy, single-storey building with a high ceiling. As the ideal is not often available, designs one and two can be built in the garden or backyard under some sort of simple shelter that will protect them from the worst of the weather. A wet kiln takes considerably more time and fuel to fire than a dry one. Also, if a wet kiln is fired too fast the escaping steam may crack the bricks. Try and site the kiln so that the firebox entrance faces away from the prevailing wind, or devise a small windbreak.

Kiln design three, the power kiln, can be built in the workshop, garage or similar building.

Your kiln may be built on the bare earth if the site is level and well-drained, but as the ground under the kiln is dried out during a firing larger, heavier kilns may subside and cause the structure to crack. Although it is not essential a concrete base for larger kilns will prove a good investment.

I make my kiln bases about 10 inches thick and as a precaution reinforce them with lengths of iron (old iron bedsteads, etc.). Then if this raft should crack it will not move, which prevents any damage to the kiln.

To stop the concrete from sucking up water from the ground I make my base on top of strong plastic sheeting, which acts as a damp course.

Kiln plans

These plans present three basic kiln designs that have been proven to fire well and are both easy and inexpensive to build. I have drawn these plans just denoting the practical limits of the fuels, fireboxes, flues, chimneys, and other relevant dimensions. This is so that within these limits you can draw upon the plans, using the components and dimensions that suit your requirements, and producing a kiln the size you want which uses the fuel you prefer.

Metric measurements for kilns

During this transition period between imperial and metric measurements it is difficult to know whether to quote the kiln measurements in feet and inches or metres and centimetres. I have used imperial measurements because as yet most people are happier with this system.

One inch = 2.54 centimetres
One foot = 30.48 centimetres

Design 1: through-draught kiln for wood, oil or gas firing

The through-draught kiln's firebox is built beneath the kiln chamber, which enables the flames to pass easily from the firebox into the pack of pots. The firebox also heats the kiln chamber by radiation through the kiln floor. This all makes for an efficient kiln that fires quickly using a relatively small amount of fuel.

A small kiln of one to four cubic feet using one or two kiln shelves in place of an arch can be built in a few hours. For larger kilns a catenary arch has to be built to span the chamber, as even if you could obtain kiln shelves large enough to span a wide chamber, they would not withstand the stress of firing.

This design works well with kilns that have a chamber of up to 15 cubic feet—for example, chamber packing space which is $2\frac{1}{2}$ ft high, $2\frac{1}{2}$ ft deep and $2\frac{1}{2}$ ft wide at its base. If you wish to build a larger kiln of this type I would recommend reading F. Olsen's *The Kiln Book* (second edition), in which he gives details of a twin firebox version of this design. (See book list, p. 141.)

This small wood fired kiln (design 1) was built by Paul Hopwood

Notes for through-draught kiln Design 1

Firebox (*B*): The length of the firebox is dictated by the length of the kiln chamber. For all sizes of oil-fired kilns the depth of the firebox should be between 9 to 12 inches. For wood firing there should be about 8 to 10 inches below the firebars and about 6 to 9 inches above. The firebars should be at least $\frac{1}{2}$ inch round steel and should be fitted 4 to 5 inches apart so that they can be replaced should they burn out. A good alternative to steel bars is a steel foot scraper-mat.

In the smaller kilns the firebox will be the same width as the kiln chamber, from 12 to 18 inches. As a firebox 18 inches wide is large enough to fire a kiln of fifteen cubic feet, it need not be built any wider than this. See Plans 1C and 1D.

The kiln shelf which forms the base to the chimney (I) takes part of the chimney weight, whilst spanning the firebox entrance. To help support it you can place under the shelf a 3 inch wide, $\frac{3}{8}$ inch thick steel strip that spans the firebox opening.

Kiln chamber (*A*): If you wish to build a kiln chamber wider than that which a kiln shelf will span (in practice this is about 20 inches) a catenary arch will have to be built, and an arch former made (see page 95).

The exit from the firebox to the chamber (J) should be 6 inches to 8 inches wide. The exit from the chamber to the chimney (G) is more crucial. For small oil or gas fired kilns of one to ten cubic feet this should be 3×6 inches to 6×6 inches. For larger oil and gas fired

In kiln design 1 a brick ledge has been made to hold the heavy steel bars which form the grate.

kilns of up to 15 cubic feet capacity an opening of 6×9 inches is necessary.

As a wood firing creates more fumes (gases and smoke) a wood kiln needs a larger exit from the chamber to the chimney, if the kiln is not to become choked during firing. I would make the exit for wood kilns fifty per cent larger than I would if the fuel were gas or oil.

In all cases I would recommend making this exit hole a little on the large size. If you find that the heat is being pulled too quickly out of the chamber you can alleviate this by sliding the chimney damper in a little

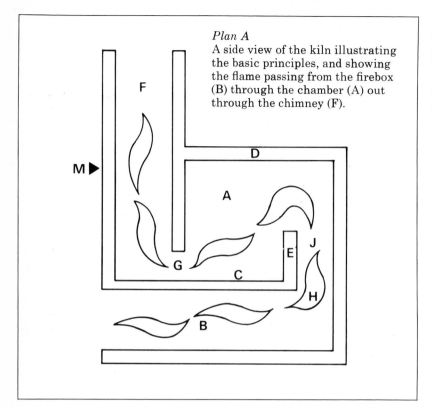

Plan A
A side view of the kiln illustrating the basic principles, and showing the flame passing from the firebox (B) through the chamber (A) out through the chimney (F).

Figure 5 Kiln design 1: plans A–F
These plans show the general principle of the through-draught kiln for both the flat roof and catenary arch versions. The depth of the firebox will vary depending on whether the kiln is wood, oil or gas fired.

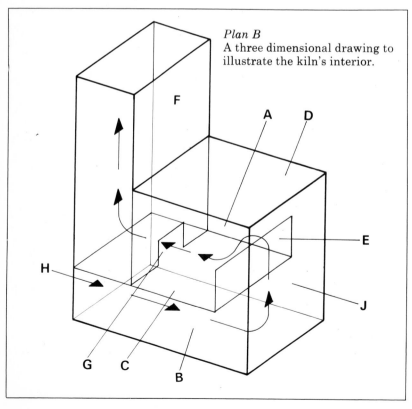

Plan B
A three dimensional drawing to illustrate the kiln's interior.

KEY

A Kiln chamber – packing space
B Firebox
C Kiln floor
D Roof – kiln shelf or catenary arch
E Bag wall, to deflect flames upwards
F Chimney
G Exit from kiln chamber to chimney
H Flame path
I Kiln shelf for base of chimney
J Exit from firebox to chamber
M Position for damper
N Secondary air holes for oil or gas firing version of this kiln
O Opening for oil or gas burner
P Fire bars for wood fired kilns

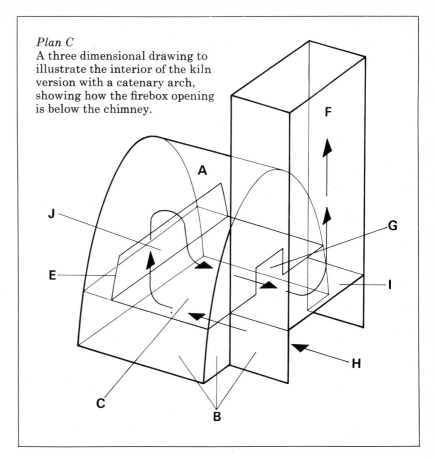

Plan C
A three dimensional drawing to illustrate the interior of the kiln version with a catenary arch, showing how the firebox opening is below the chimney.

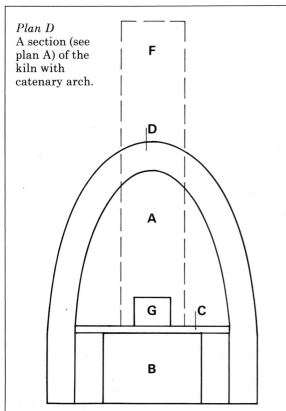

Plan D
A section (see plan A) of the kiln with catenary arch.

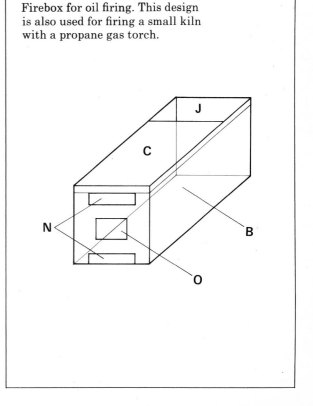

Plan E
Firebox for oil firing. This design is also used for firing a small kiln with a propane gas torch.

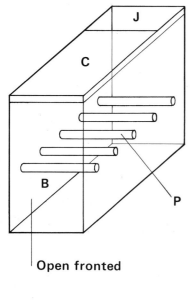

Plan F
Wood fired firebox showing fire bars.

J

C

B

P

Open fronted

Kiln chimney (*F*): The chimney should be 9 inches square internally and stand approximately three times as high as the kiln chamber. When using a forced air oil burner powered by a blower, vacuum cleaner or compressor then a chimney of only about twice the height of the kiln chamber is necessary. The same is true when a propane burner is used.

The whole chimney may be built of bricks, but if you wish when the chimney is 2 feet above the top of the arch it may be made of steel tube. Changing from a square to a circular horizontal cross-section has the effect of tapering the chimney. This is ideal as a tapered chimney increases the speed of the draught. A chimney built wholly of bricks should be slightly restricted by corbelling the brickwork in by 2 inches about half way up. To control the 'pull' of the chimney it is necessary to build into it a horizontal sliding kiln shelf to act as a damper (M). See photo, p. 94.

It is also easier at a later date to close up this hole than to enlarge it.

The job of the bagwall (E) is to force the flames up into the chamber. The ideal height for the bagwall is about half that of the chamber. If you notice that the pots at the top of the kiln chamber are coming out under-fired the bagwall can be built up by one or two bricks, and the reverse applies if you notice that the base of the kiln pack is under-firing. Then the bagwall requires lowering.

As you can see from the plan of the catenary arch version (1D) of this kiln the brick up door has to be placed at the bagwall end of the kiln. After packing the kiln the few bricks that make up the bagwall have to be replaced before the door is bricked up.

Design 2: down-draught kiln for oil firing

I have built several kilns of this design with kiln chambers from ten to forty cubic feet. I feel that for a medium-sized oil-fired kiln it is a far from perfect design, but having looked at many medium-sized oil-fired kilns I have yet to see a better one. Every new kiln I have built of this type has had firing characteristics all of its own. The first firing was often a disappointment with pots over- and under-fired, but after building up or lowering the bagwall (E), or increasing or decreasing the flue setting (L) the subsequent firings have

Figure 6 Kiln design 2: plans A–C
Down-draught oil fired kiln for
both stoneware and earthenware
firings. This is an ideal kiln for
use in conjunction with the oil
burning system described on p. 102

KEY
A Kiln chamber – packing space
B Firebox
C Floor, of solid heavy firebrick
D Arch
E Bag wall
F Chimney
F(2) Alternative position for
      chimney
G Exit from flue (L) to chimney
   (F)
L Flue and flue setting
M Damper
N Secondary air for burner
O Burner opening
S Bottom shelf of kiln

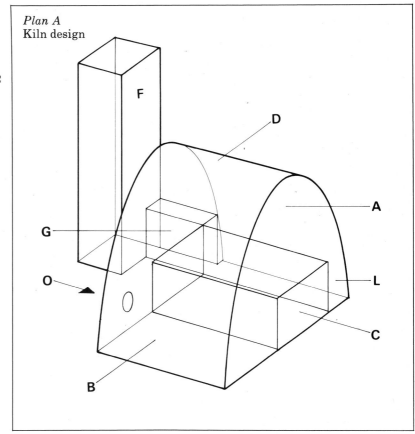

Plan A
Kiln design

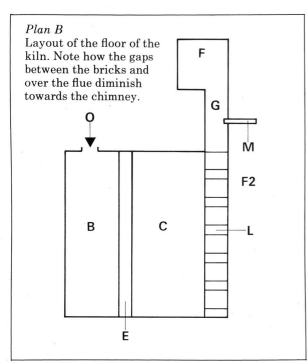

Plan B
Layout of the floor of the
kiln. Note how the gaps
between the bricks and
over the flue diminish
towards the chimney.

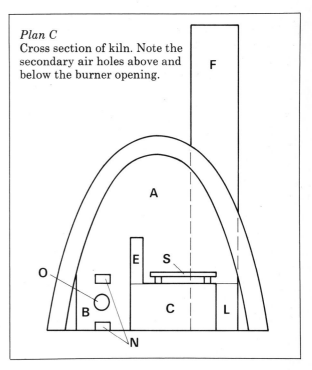

Plan C
Cross section of kiln. Note the
secondary air holes above and
below the burner opening.

got better and better, and a completely uniform firing was always achieved the third or fourth time.

Most potters have one or two glazes that require a higher or lower temperature than the rest of their glazes, so for them an ideal kiln is one that will fire consistently with an area in the chamber that is ten to twenty degrees centigrade hotter or cooler than the rest of the pack. I have lowered the bagwall of my own kiln by two bricks. The bottom third of my kiln pack is fired to 1280°C while the top two-thirds reaches about 1260°C. This arrangement is ideal for my range of glazes.

The series of photographs on pp. 92–4 show John Beattie in his workshop building the down-draught oil-fired kiln shown in Design 2. The base was built of heavy firebrick and the kiln chamber of light IFB firebrick. This is a large version of this kiln with a packing space of about forty cubic feet. John used 750 IFB firebricks and 200 hard firebricks, which he bought second-hand: they were in good condition and cost him about 20% of the new price. As he had plenty of cheap IFBs he also used these for the outside insulating skin. The inside of the kiln was covered with a $1\frac{1}{2}$ inch layer of hot face ceramic fibre tiles.

The kiln's burner is a Swirlamiser, (Denver-type low-pressure burner) which is commercially-made. It is very similar in design and operation to the unit described on pp. 102–4.

Notes for down-draught kiln design 2

Kiln chamber (*A*): This design is suitable for building a kiln with a chamber as small as ten cubic feet or as large as forty cubic feet. Always build your kiln to suit the materials and kiln furniture that are available. As far as you can, try to make kiln dimensions equal; a kiln chamber should preferably be as wide at its base as it is deep and high. At first the bagwall (E) should be built about one-third as high as the chamber, and later adjusted up or down, or staggered according to how the kiln fires. If the bottom of the chamber is under-firing, lower the bagwall. If the top is under-firing build the bagwall up. Should the back or the front of the kiln pack be under-firing the bagwall can be staggered to adjust this.

The floor block (C) should be 12 to 15 inches deep, creating a flue (L) this deep and 4 to 6 inches wide. The flue is partially blocked off with bricks, creating a range of staggered gaps $\frac{1}{2}$ inch to 3 inches in dimension. These should be wider furthest away from the burner, so that the flame is pulled to the far corner of the kiln.

The exit from the flue to the chimney (G) is as wide and deep as the flue. This is the best place for the damper. A vertical slot is made in the brick work, so that a kiln shelf can act as a damper (M) to restrict the chimney's pull.

Firebox (*B*): The depth of the firebox is created by the floor (C) 12 inches to 15 inches. For all sizes of kiln a 9 inch wide firebox gives enough space for combustion.

Above and below the burner opening (O) there should be two openings (N) to provide secondary air to help the oil burn cleanly. These should be about 4 by 6 inches each.

Chimney (*F*): The chimney should be about twice as high as the kiln chamber. For kilns with a chamber of up to twenty-five cubic feet it should be at least 9 inches square. Kilns above this size will need a 12 inch square chimney. The chimney can be built wholly of bricks or bricks can be used for the first four feet and the remainder can be constructed of steel tubing. (See photo, p. 94.) A tapering chimney increases the speed of the draught, and if you use circular steel tubing at the top of the stack, the transition from square brickwork to steel tubing enhances this effect. A stack built wholly of bricks can be reduced in cross-section by two inches halfway up to achieve the same result.

Plan 2B shows an alternative position for the chimney (F2) where the damper passage (G) leaves the kiln at right angles to the kiln chamber. I have shown this alternative because if your kiln site lacks space it may be more suitable to build the chimney in this position.

Kiln building: designs 1 and 2

To refresh your memory and help you avoid small needless errors during the building of your kiln you may find it useful, when using the following instructions, to refer back occasionally to the section on choice of kiln, pp. 79–83.

Stage 1: your plan

When you have decided on the design and size of kiln you wish to build the first step is to make a detailed plan of your own. Make sure that this contains all the relevant details listed below.

Measurements

List all measurements. Ideally kilns should be built of whole and half bricks. This is less wasteful and saves time—cutting bricks can be hard work.

When designing the chamber the size of the kiln shelves must be taken into account. A one inch gap should be left between the shelf and the kiln wall. Don't do as a friend of mine did. He built his kiln with a chamber with a floor area on which to pack shelves of 15×24 inches and then bought some excellent second-hand shelves measuring 17×10 inches. There was no way he could use them, two deep or singly. So obtain your shelves before building your kiln.

Door

The door should be made a few inches wider than the shelves and in a position so that the shelves can be easily placed in the chamber.

Spy holes

One or two spy holes $1\frac{1}{2}$ inch square should be made in either the chamber wall or door. I fire my kilns only by pyrometric cones; I find it useful to have two sets of these, so I have two spy holes, one in the middle front and the other roughly in the centre back of the kiln chamber.

Stage 2: kiln site

The next step is to prepare the kiln site by making a base, and if necessary some form of shelter. Assemble all of your materials on site. These will comprise:

Bricks for the hot face and outer skins. (If you are to make a catenary arch of heavy firebrick, approximately 40% of the arch bricks will have to be of a tapered type. IFBs can be easily cut and rubbed into shape so it is not essential that these are tapered.)

Making the catenary arch former from 1 inch chip board and 2 × 1 inch softwood.

Kiln base, made of heavy firebricks.

Arch former on kiln base. This is put on wedges so it can easily be removed when the arch is completed.

Laying arch bricks. You have to find the best arrangement of standard and arch bricks to cover the former.

Aluminium foil between the hot face and second layer of bricks helps to insulate the kiln.

The arch with the former removed. The second layer of insulation bricks are being laid.

Top of arch. Note the configuration of the tapered arch bricks. Every size of arch will have a slightly different arrangement of bricks.

Kiln with front and back walls in place with a brick up door. The door bricks should fit tightly and be numbered so they can be put back in the correct place for each firing.

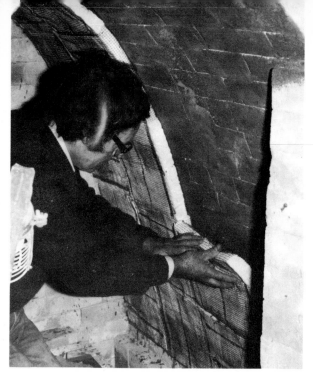

John Beattie sticking ceramic fibre tiles to the hot face of the kiln. These decrease the kiln's fuel consumption by over 30%, but they are expensive—you will have to balance the cost with that of the fuel saving before deciding to use them on your kiln.

Base of chimney and damper. Note the transition from brick work to steel tube for the chimney.

Kiln shelves and some kiln furniture.

Fireclay, for mortar.

Tools—trowel, hammer, brick cutting chisel, level, bow saw and spare blades, tape measure.

Stage 3: arch former

If you want to make a catenary arch kiln, you will need an arch former. Before you start it may be profitable to enquire with fellow potters in your area if they have, or know of, a suitable former.

If you can't get hold of one, timber will have to be purchased: a sheet or sheets of plywood or chipboard to make the ends of the arch former and lathing strips for the rails that support the bricks. (See photo p. 92)

To make a catenary arch, hang a fine link chain in a loop on the vertical plywood. When the loop is adjusted to form an arch of the correct depth and width you pin the chain in place at its ends. Then spray the loop with aerosol paint, which will leave an outline. Now draw a line one inch inside the outline and cut the arch shape out with a hand saw or jig saw on the inner line. This inch is to allow for the 2 × 1 inch rails. Using the first arch shape as a pattern cut a second piece of plywood. Clad the two plywood shapes with the lathing strips that have been cut to the depth of the kiln. The side rails should be spaced about two inches apart. The top rails should be butted together and planed to regain the catenary shape.

The arch former in the photograph on p. 92 is fairly long and has been supported in the centre with a third blockboard shape. The one hundred heavy fire bricks that it takes to build a

This oil fired kiln was built by students on the Medway College of Design's kiln site. It is based on kiln design 2.

medium size arch weigh about nine hundred pounds.

The length of the chain you use to draw your arch shape will give you an instant guide to how many bricks you will need. For example, if your length of chain is 72 inches, your bricks 3 inches deep and the depth of the arch is four bricks, the sum adds up like this:
$72 \div 3 = 24 \times 4 = 96$ bricks.
Add 10% of this total to compensate for the tapered arch brick to give a total of 106 bricks for the arch.

Stage 4: bricklaying

Bricklaying for building small and medium size kilns is not difficult but before embarking upon kiln building

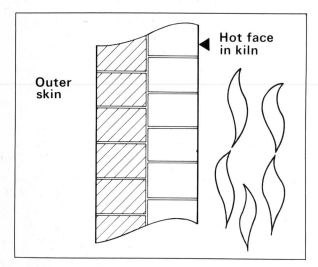

Figure 7 Kiln brickwork. The kiln brickwork should be laid so that there are no through joints from the hot face to the outer insulating skin. A leaky kiln uses a lot more fuel.

proper it is a useful precaution to lay one or two courses of bricks out on the base. This is to make sure your paper plan will work out in reality.

When required, IFBs can be cut with a bow saw and made to fit exactly by rubbing two bricks together. An easy and quick method of shaping IFBs is to rub them on a concrete building block. A mortar of coarse fireclay or fireclay and sand may be used, though IFBs can be laid without mortar, if carefully fitted. As heavy fire bricks have to be cut with a brick chisel and cannot be rubbed square, a little mortar is required to lay them level. The mortar is here used just for levelling and only binds the bricks together loosely.

Lay a course of heavy fire brick to form the kiln base. Then place the catenary arch former in position on the base. The former is placed on four small wedges so that it can be removed when the arch is built.

As you can see from the photograph on p. 93, the arch is made from a combination of tapered and straight

bricks, the top section being made wholly of tapered bricks. Before laying the bricks on the former proper, play around with an assortment of tapered and straight bricks to determine the best arrangement. It is important that all the tapered bricks point inwards and that the key brick at the top of the arch is a taper. As shown in the photographs of the kilns the bricks should be laid in order so that they overlap, in order that no long vertical cracks are created.

You now remove the arch former by taking out its wedges and sliding it out, being careful that it does not disturb the arch. All being well you will now be able to stand back and admire your handiwork. To its maker the bare arch will look beautiful.

Complete the kiln to your plan with its firebox, floor, flue, back and front walls complete with a brick up door. The back and front hot face walls should be built within the arch, with the bricks cut so they fit tightly into the arch. Any small gaps can be filled with mortar. The outer insulating skin of bricks or blocks is built round and over the kiln. A layer of aluminium cooking foil placed between the hot face and the insulating bricks will improve the insulating properties of the kiln. Single skin kilns made of high temperature insulation bricks can be insulated with just a single layer of low temperature ceramic fibre blanket. This can be held in place by either insulation board or chicken wire.

Make at least two spy holes ($1\frac{1}{2} \times 1\frac{1}{2}$ inches) with an easily removable brick plug. Place these at the back and front of the kiln. I build as many as four spy holes into my kilns. When I have become familiar with a kiln's firing pattern I block off three of them and place my pyrometric cones behind the centre spy hole at the front of the chamber. The chimney should now be built, with either a brick base and a steel tubing top section, or all of bricks.

Brick making

Depending on the availability of suitable materials it can be an easy and inexpensive matter to make your own high temperature insulating bricks, and outer skin insulating blocks.

High temperature insulating bricks (IFBs)

> Recipe by volume. Fire to 1200 to 1300°C.
>
> China clay   1 part
> Saw dust   1 part
> Water to make into a stiff mix.

On firing the sawdust burns out, leaving a porous brick, about 15% smaller than the unfired brick. If you have available any old fired-out IFB bricks these can be crushed and added to the above mix. If twenty to fifty per cent old IFBs are added the shrinkage when fired will be considerably reduced. Inexpensive clean second grade china clay can be bought in one or two ton loads as dug direct from most china clay pits. As transport charges are high this only becomes viable if you live within easy reach of the clay pits. My local joinery workshop is always knee-deep in sawdust and they are only too grateful if anyone is willing to take some away.

If you do not already have the use of a kiln you are faced with a 'catch 22' problem of how to make kiln bricks to build a kiln if you don't have a kiln to fire them in. The potter Mike Dodd overcame this problem by building his kiln 'raw'. He built a kiln with a hot face skin of unfired china clay, and sawdust bricks. When the kiln was fired cracks did appear in the brickwork but were easily repaired, and the kiln was successfully fired many times.

Brick moulds in two sizes:
9 × 9 × 4½ inches, and 6 × 9 × 18 inches.

Insulating and outer skin insulating block made in the first mould.

Outer skin insulating blocks

Recipe by volume

Any ball clay	$4\frac{1}{2}$ parts
Coal cinders or coal ash	$4\frac{1}{2}$ parts
Cement	1 part

These are not fired, but dried in the sun, or on a concrete floor. When dry this mix has very high insulating properties.

My central heating boiler which gives me an endless supply of coal ash and a stock of ball clay that I no longer use for pots, provides me with the materials for cheap insulation blocks. Other mixes such as chopped straw, clay and cement will also suffice. Use what is available but keep the cement content of the brick low otherwise it will not withstand the firing.

When making these recipes the amounts can be measured by bucketsful, and be mixed with a spade, as you do when making concrete. Of course a concrete mixer is a great help in this operation. A sanded wooden frame $6 \times 9 \times 18$ inches or $9 \times 9 \times 4\frac{1}{2}$ inches is used as a mould; I have found these sizes most convenient for kiln building. If the mix is fairly stiff the mould may be removed immediately from the brick and be used repeatedly.

Mortar for exterior brickwork

Lime	10 parts
Sand	30 parts
Cement	1 part

This weatherproof mortar can be used for laying the kiln's chimney bricks and the outer skin insulation bricks or blocks. It cannot be used for the inner skin bricklaying as it will not withstand high temperatures.

Kiln furniture

In the past most potters fired their ware in saggars, made of fire clay and grog. Nowadays most potters prefer to fire their pots in an open pack on kiln shelves. I have experimented with making shelves but only those which are some three inches thick have withstood stoneware temperatures.

As shelves this thick are very wasteful of kiln space I now use 1 inch commercially made shelves. Second-hand kiln furniture can be found through the classified advertisements in pottery magazines, and if there are any industrial potteries or ceramic tile manufacturers in your area these are well worth investigating. Kiln props can be expensive; a good alternative can be a selection of cut and uncut $2 \times 4\frac{1}{2} \times 9$ inch heavy firebricks. To level the shelves on the bricks I use small pads of plastic fireclay.

The art of kiln firing: designs 1 and 2

You should avoid firing on windy days, as a high wind will not allow the chimney to pull freely. If your kiln is sited in a built-up area have a thought for your neighbours, and don't start the smoky reduction firing on a sunny Sunday afternoon.

My previous pottery was in the centre of a village. The kiln was surrounded by private dwellings and therefore I always timed it so the later stages of the stoneware reduction firings (when smoke was created) took place well after dusk. Adopting this strategy I fired my large oil kiln regularly over a period of six years without complaint.

The problems of firing a new kiln

A new unfired kiln contains a lot of water in the bricks and mortar, and I suggest you slowly fire the empty kiln to a few hundred degrees to dry it out. As long as you do not get over eager there is no reason why it cannot be commissioned full of pots. If the kiln is fired too quickly the trapped water boils and cracks the bricks and mortar when escaping.

Some years ago I built a 100 cubic foot kiln with a firebox of 'heavies' and the chamber of IFBs. After packing my 'pride and joy' with pots, bricking up the door and sealing the cracks with fireclay slip, I warmed it up to about 100°C for ten hours. I was then satisfied that it was thoroughly dry and started to increase the temperature. When about 400°C was reached I could see that the bricks were spitting little pieces all over the pots. I stopped firing, let the kiln cool down and unpacked and cleaned it out. Luckily I had noticed in time and little damage had been done to the pots or the kiln.

After this episode I experimented and found that my kiln bricks had contained between a quarter and half a pint of water each; my kiln's inner skin of 1000 bricks had therefore held about forty gallons of water. On refiring, the kiln was thoroughly dry and everything went well.

Adjusting the kiln

When unpacking your first glaze firing make careful notes of how the pots have fired in the various parts of the chamber. If the kiln has fired unevenly, the problem can usually be remedied for the next firing by adjusting the bagwall. Building up the bagwall will induce heat to the top of the chamber, whereas lowering it will allow heat to the exit flue more quickly, making the base of the pack hotter and reducing the temperature at the top of the chamber.

A common and a most depressing occurrence on a first firing is a complete failure to reach maximum temperature. When this happens the kiln usually sticks stubbornly one or two hundred degrees below the maximum temperature.

If the fuel is burning well in the fire box but the temperature refusing to rise you have probably made the exit flue (or in the case of Kiln Design 2, the gaps in the flue setting) too large, and the heat is being pulled out of the chamber. This can usually be remedied during firing by closing the chimney damper a little. Even if this does work, you should restrict the exit flue or flue setting a little after the firing.

A kiln may fail to reach maximum temperature because it is choking (that is the fire in the firebox is not burning cleanly). If this happens, the secondary air holes to the firebox may be enlarged to induce a brighter flame, and the exit flue or flue setting gaps should be enlarged to allow the gases to escape more quickly. The chimney should be built up by two or three feet to produce more pull on the firebox.

When firing larger kilns the fire in the firebox can be very lazy when first lit, almost refusing to burn. This is because the chimney is cold and so is not yet pulling. In this case it will be necessary to light a small fire in the base of the chimney. When building a large kiln I leave two loose bricks at the base of the chimney for this purpose, and when the fire is pulling well in the firebox I replace the chimney bricks and temporarily seal over the cracks with fireclay—a leaky chimney does not pull well.

Wood firing

The art of wood firing a kiln is to gradually build up the fire so that the temperature is increased without interruption. It is impossible to estimate beforehand how much wood it will take to fire any particular kiln. The determining factors are the size of the kiln, the size of the firebox, the maximum temperature required, whether reduction is required or not, and the skill of the fireman. All I can say is that for a small kiln you should have four or five carloads of wood on site. Our local saw mill sells its slab wood in bundles; one of these weighs approximately $\frac{3}{4}$ ton, enough timber for several firings of a small or medium-sized kiln. Softwood is ideal, and pine is the best of all, as it burns fast, clean and hot. The wood should be dry, and cut into thin lengths suitable for your firebox. Wood only burns on its surface; thin pieces of wood burn quickly as they present more of their volume to the fire than do large logs.

I start the fire on the floor of the firebox. When this is going well I place a few pieces of wood above it on the fire bars and the fire is soon transferred onto fire bars. The next endeavour is to keep the fire burning fierce and bright. Over-stoking will smother the fire and cause a temperature drop. Every so often the ashes should be raked over with a long steel bar to make sure that all of the charcoal is being burnt, but the ash should not be raked out as it radiates a great deal of heat. The thinnest and driest of your wood should be kept for the latter stages of your firing, as this is when you will need the hottest flames. A pyrometer can be very reassuring during firing as if the needle is constantly rising you know your stoking technique is working.

Wood firing usually creates a very slight reducing atmosphere; should you wish to increase this the chimney damper can be pushed in, and/or the front bottom of the firebox can be closed up a little, by means of a few bricks. Over-reduction can slow down or stop the temperature climb. If this happens reduction should be decreased. With some large wood fired kilns reduction has to be given in bursts as they refuse to reduce and gain temperature at the same time. With dry thin wood and a good firing technique you should not encounter this problem with small and medium-sized kilns.

If you wish your pots to be heavily flashed and toasted with wood ash, towards the end of the firing the ashes under the fire bars should be raked and stirred. When the firing is completed cover the open entrance to the firebox with a dry kiln shelf or close it with dry bricks. This will stop the kiln cooling too quickly.

The length of the firing depends very much on the individual potter's needs and the vagaries of the kiln. A description of a typical firing schedule can be seen on pages 73–5.

In conclusion, I can say that wood firing is hard work. If there is a good supply of cheap wood in your area, I feel it is well worth the effort, as wood firing can give pots an extra-special quality that makes all the preparation and stoking worth while.

Oil firing

Before the 1970's oil crisis oil was by far the most convenient and cheap source of kiln fuel. The subsequent incredible rise in price still does not rule it out as a viable kiln fuel, however. Even now the cost of firing my oil kiln amounts to less than 8% of the value of the fired pots.

Making an oil burning system
There are many commercially-made oil burning systems. This simple system can easily be put together

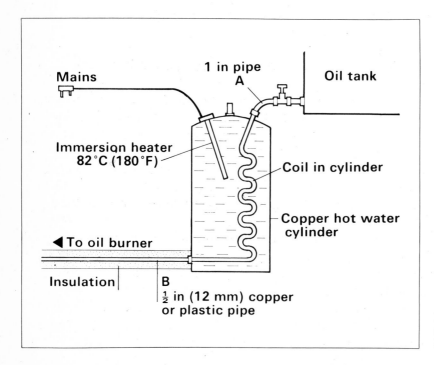

Figure 8 Pre-heating system for sump oil. Details of this system are given on page 107

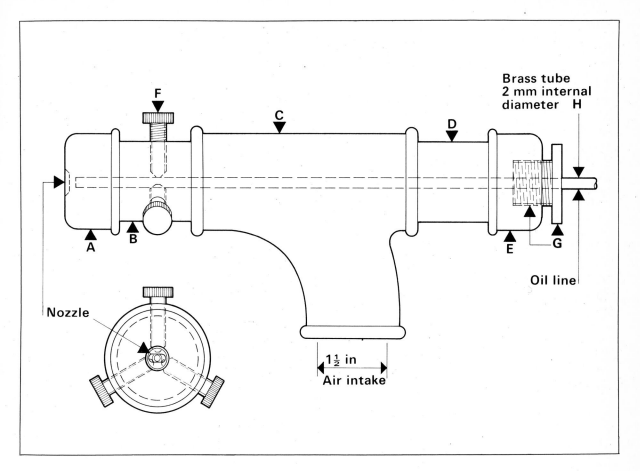

Figure 9 This simple oil burner is made from standard pipe fittings available from plumbing supply.

Oil burner

Nozzle end of oil burner.

and works as well as any of them, and better than most.

It is designed to burn central heating oil (gas oil) or when used with a preheating device as shown in Fig. 8, with waste sump oil (drain oil). See page 107 also.

As you can see from the photograph the burner is made from five parts of cast iron $1\frac{1}{2}$ inch pipe fittings, a thin brass tube and four bolts. The oil is gravity fed to the burner from an oil drum by means of a plastic pipe. The oil flow is controlled by a small clamp on the oil line. A forced air supply is provided to the burner by a cylinder vacuum cleaner. The vacuum cleaner's air line is fitted to the 'blow' end of the machine and to the air intake of the burner. Inside the burner, the the forced air passes over the oil pipe, catching the oil as it leaves the brass pipe at the end of the burner and blows it into the kiln in the form of a fine vapour.

The parts of the burner can be bought from your local plumber or builders' merchant. Second-hand cylinder vacuum cleaners are to be found for very little cost in junkshops or flea markets. Although I always keep a spare vacuum cleaner I have yet to be let down by this very inexpensive system. An equivalent commercially-made burner system costs several hundreds of pounds (or dollars).

Parts required:

$1\frac{1}{2}$ inch internal diameter steel pipe fittings *
2 caps (Parts A and E, as shown on Figure 9)
2 pieces of threaded pipe $2\frac{1}{2}$ inches long (Parts B and D)
1 T junction (Part C)
1 brass tube 13 inches long—internal diameter $\frac{1}{12}$ inch (2 mm) (Part H)
3 bolts $1\frac{1}{2}$ inches long—$\frac{1}{4}$ inch thread (Part F)
1 adjustment screw (Part G). This is a large fine-threaded screw which enables the oil tube to be adjusted backwards or forwards.

 * At the time of writing a metric equivalent of $1\frac{1}{2}$ inch cast iron pipe fittings is not available in Britain. If in the future only metric fittings are available, use the equivalent size or larger. A smaller bore will decrease the efficiency of the burner.

Stage 1: Cut an elliptical hole $\frac{3}{10} \times \frac{1}{5}$ inch in the centre of the face of the cap Part A. This is done by drilling and enlarging with a small round file. The front face of the hole is countersunk out to $\frac{1}{2}$ inch.

Stage 2: Drill three holes in Part B and tap to fit bolts, Part F. The bolts point in towards the centre of the burner to hold the oil tube, Part H, in place.

Stage 3: Drill and tap end cap, Part E, so that large bolt, Part G, screws into it.

Drill a hole down the length of Part G to fit brass pipe, Part H. This should be silver soldered or welded in place. This adjustment screw should allow the oil tube to be moved tight up to the inside face of the burner front, Part A, and also allow it to be moved back from the inside face at least $\frac{1}{3}$ inch. The exit end of the oil tube should be reduced on a lathe or alternatively, by means of a small hammer, from a diameter of $\frac{1}{8}$ to $\frac{1}{16}$ inch. This helps the oil to flow smoothly, as reducing the bore ensures that there is adequate pressure at the burner nozzle.

Stage 4: Assemble burner as shown in Fig. 10. If you do not have the facilities to carry out some of the work on the burner, your local school's metalwork department, blacksmith or small engineering workshop should be able to help. In fact very little skill is required to make this burner.

Safety notes for oil burner
Before each firing check all equipment very carefully, ensuring that there are no oil leaks. Check that the oil line is securely clamped to the burner and oil tank, and locate the tank in a safe place well away from the kiln where it cannot be knocked over. Don't put the air and oil pipes where you can trip over them. During firing the burner gets very hot, so handle with caution when adjusting it.

Firing procedure for oil burner

The burner, oil tank, vacuum cleaner and parts are assembled as in Fig. 10. For safety the oil tank should be placed at least 10 feet away from the kiln. The tank should be 3 or 4 feet above the burner so it is fed by gravity. The oil flow is controlled by a small restricting clamp on the plastic oil line.

During the early stages of the firing the vacuum cleaner may produce too powerful a blast of air, so that the flame blows out. If this happens the problem can be overcome by making an adjustable air leak in the air hose, which is done by cutting a 1 inch hole in the hose connector at the cleaner end. The hole can be covered by varying amounts with a sliding metal or plastic collar, which dissipates the power of the vacuum cleaner.

The burner is supported in the mouth of the firebox

Figure 10 Burner set up. A second hand vacuum cleaner, an old oil drum and some plastic pipe completes this very inexpensive but efficient burner system.

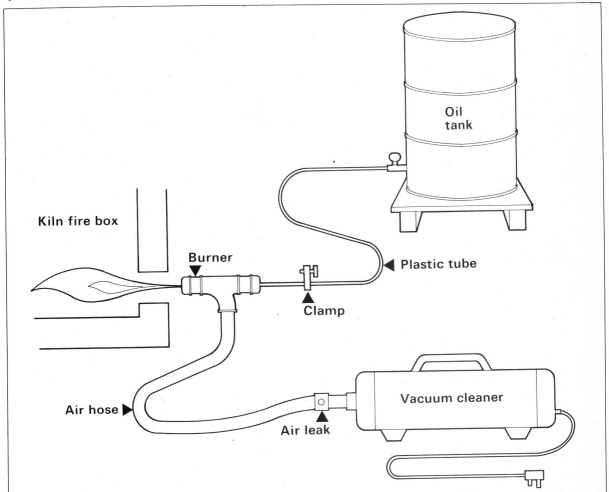

by laying it on two or three firebricks. The burner flame should be adjusted so it burns clean and bright. This is done by screwing the oil tube, Part H, backwards or forwards by means of screws, Parts G and F. The amount of oil used will vary between 4 and 40 gallons depending on the size of the kiln, and the nature of the firing, but for example, I would expect a 15 cubic foot kiln that is reduction fired to 1300°C to use between 15 to 20 gallons of gas oil.

Lighting up: The easiest way to ignite the oil vapour is by a small gas blow torch. In the early stages of firing the burner should be watched in case it goes out. After a little while the firebox will become red hot and after that the vapour is self-igniting.

Reduction oil firing: Should you wish to introduce a reduction atmosphere into the kiln chamber, it can be done in several ways: you can partially close down the secondary air holes, pushing in the chimney damper or increase the oil supply so that the flame burns slightly cloudily. When my kiln gets to its reducing temperature I use a little of all three methods, which gives an even reduction atmosphere throughout the chamber. The section giving details of once-firing shows a typical firing schedule, p. 75.

Sump oil firing

Waste sump oil or drain oil can be bought from most garages for a very small cost per gallon, and the garage owner is often happy to give it away. As well as having the advantage of low cost, its impurities can give the fired ware a warm toasted look, similar to that of wood fired pots. However, the small particles of dirt present in sump oil will block the fine jet of an oil burner unless the oil is cleaned. Also, even uncontaminated sump oil does not flow easily and would not gravity feed from an oil tank to the burner unless it were preheated.

I visit my local garage with the back of my station wagon packed full of five gallon oil drums, standing on a sheet of plastic.

I fill these drums from the garage's storage tank, placing a large funnel in the top of each oil drum in order to filter off the larger particles of dirt. When

I return to the pottery I replace the funnel filter with a finer one and place it in the top of the large storage tank (old stocking tights make good filtering material). The oil is then transferred to this tank. However careful you are this is a messy job, so do protect yourself and your car.

I devised a system to heat the sump oil so that it flows freely to the burner. I bought a second-hand copper hot water cylinder, the type that has a central heating coil in it. I placed the cylinder next to the oil storage tank and attached the top of the cylinder coil to the tank with 1 inch plastic pipe. From the bottom of the coil I ran a $\frac{1}{2}$ inch insulated copper pipe to the burner. An electrical immersion heater was fitted in the top of the cylinder, which is filled with water. The immersion heater heats the water and therefore the oil in the coil to 180°F, at which temperature the oil flows easily. As a precaution you could fit a line filter into the pipe at position 'B' to catch any remaining sediment. It is worthwhile covering the cylinder with an insulating jacket, which will help keep the temperature constant. Also insulate pipe A; this will help the flow from the storage tank. See Figure 8, p. 102.

Firing technique for sump oil

My oil burner is fed by two oil lines. Down one flows the preheated sump oil and down the other the central heating oil.

Sump oil does not ignite nearly so readily as heating oil (gas oil), so I start the firing with central heating oil. After a while the back of the firebox becomes red hot, which means that if the burner goes out it will immediately re-ignite. At this point I switch over to burning the sump oil, which then burns well. Some potters like to burn a 50–50 mix of the two oils. As I have a stop-cock on both tanks I can adjust the mix to whatever is required.

Potters use various firing methods for exploiting this cheap fuel, amongst which are to start the firing with a propane gas burner and switch over to sump oil, or in the initial stages of firing have a propane gas torch burning next to the oil burner. When the combined oil and gas have heated the firebox to red heat the gas burner can be withdrawn. (See safety notes for oil burner, page 104.)

Propane gas firing

Firing with propane gas is very convenient and presents very few problems. The equipment is not complicated and is easy to use; just a blow torch (as in the photograph on page 139) and cylinders of gas.

Propane firing for the basic kiln designs 1 and 2 is relatively expensive. Design 3 has been specifically designed for propane firing and uses this fuel very economically. Other than cost the only drawback of propane firing is that if you draw the gas off too quickly it will freeze. The cylinder can be thawed by pouring water over it, but during this operation the temperature in the kiln will be dropping. This means that except with the smallest of kilns, propane kilns must be fired from a series of three or four cylinders that are plumbed together so that a small quantity of gas is taken from each of them at any one time. Of course, this all adds to the cost of propane firing.

Reduction for high temperature propane firings is controlled in the same way as for an oil fired kiln, that is, by the secondary air, the burner, and the chimney damper.

Safety notes for kiln building and firing

If treated with respect kilns should hold no dangers. At all times when firing your kiln remember the heat it contains. Remember the possibility of burns from hot burners and fireboxes. When building your kiln make sure it is well away from anything inflammable, and make sure your kiln has several feet of clearance above it so roof joists are not endangered.

Be careful when looking into spy holes during firing. As a precaution I always wear special dark goggles. The hard work of wood firing can make one very hot. A few salt tablets and plenty of long drinks can save the stoker a bad headache the next day.

See also safety notes for the oil burner, page 104.

Design 3:
the power kiln

Utilising the modern high insulation materials ceramic fibre and block with a pressurised fuel, a new breed of super-efficient kiln can be built.

Kiln design 3 is fired using propane gas, and can be reduction fired if desired. It does not have an external chimney and can be safely fired in a workshop, garage or similar building. The design I have given here has an internal size of about five cubic feet, but with more powerful burners it can be built up to three times larger.

I became interested in these small fast firing kilns when I saw the quality of the fired pots from David Leach's one cubic foot kiln. He had built this of block held together by an asbestos and steel frame, and fired it with a small propane blow torch burner. In this simple structure he has glaze fired

porcelain in less than four hours and has once-fired raw glazed porcelain in about five hours. This small kiln was remarkably economical, firing up to eight times from a small tank of propane gas. David has been so pleased with his small kiln he has now built a six cubic foot version.

My fast fire kiln was designed using David Leach's experiences as a basis and a great deal of help from Ray Scott, the supplier of block and ceramic fibre in England.

As the concept of the kiln is radically different from traditional kilns I have included extra notes on the construction, and firing. The general notes in the book on kiln choice, building, and so on all apply, although the new materials do provide some exceptions to the rule.

I cannot overstate how simple it is to make this kiln. Building it demands no specific skills, only a little love and care.

Materials for power kiln (five cubic foot version)

Steel frame, see Fig. 11
2 steel rods $31 \times \frac{1}{4}$ inches.
2 sheets of 8×4 ft $\times \frac{1}{4}$ inch calcium silicate.
80 blocks $9 \times 4\frac{1}{2} \times 3$ inches.
1 ceramic fibre board box chimney section, $9 \times 4 \times 27$ inches.
1 high temperature insulation brick beam 1400 grade $9 \times 3 \times 27$ inches.
12 ft of 1 ft 6 inch wide, 2 mm thick ceramic fibre paper
12 ft 6 inches of 2 ft wide $\frac{1}{2}$ inch thick ceramic fibre blanket 1250 grade
12 ft 6 inches of 2 ft wide 1 inch thick ceramic fibre blanket 1400 grade.
$3\frac{1}{2}$ pts (2 litres) of ceramic fibre adhesive.
2 ceramic fibre board blocks 1400 grade, $6 \times 2 \times 6$ inch.
2 pieces of kanthal wire 12 inches long.
2 propane burners, vertical 9000 BTU each with fail-safe device, and 12 ft of tubing.
1 bottle of propane gas 42 lb (19 kilos) or larger with regulator.
U.S. suppliers of ceramic fiber, (Kaowool) and other refractory materials are: Babcock and Wilcox, P.O. Box 923, Augusta, GA 30903 or A. P. Green, 1018 E. Breckenridge St., Mexico, MO65265.

Notes for Fig. 11, power kiln frame

The frame for my kiln was made at my local forge from scrap welded $1\frac{1}{2}$ inch steel angle iron. The price for such a job can vary considerably so it is prudent to obtain several quotes. I had considered making the frame from drilled industrial shelving angle iron, which can be bolted together, but purchased new this would have cost me much more than the professional-looking welded frame. However, scrap merchants often have shelving angle iron, and they could be well worth investigating.

Kiln frame with base sheet in place. Two 3 inch burner holes are cut in the sheet $5\frac{1}{2}$ inches in from the burner rail end of the sheet, (see Fig. 11) and $7\frac{1}{2}$ inches in from the sides. This is covered with a piece of the $\frac{1}{2}$ inch thick 1250 blanket.

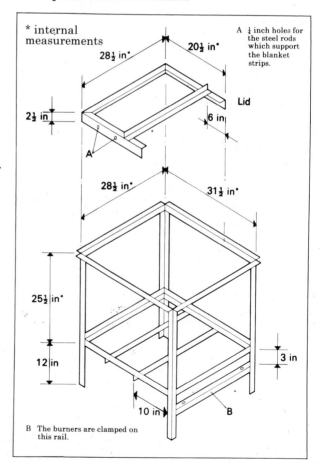

Figure 11 The power kiln frame

Method of constructing the power kiln

The kiln's steel frame is lined with calcium-silicate sheets, which is the safe substitute for asbestos.

No mortar is used to bed down the blocks; instead strips of ceramic fiber paper are placed between the brick joints. It is important that the bricks fit well, as any irregularities may cause the brickwork to crack during firing. These bricks are easily shaped by a file or by rubbing them together, and they are easily cut by a hand saw. Do not use a good saw as it will wear.

Between the bricks and the calcium-silicate sheets a half inch layer of ceramic fibre blanket is placed. This is held on to the sheets by the blanket adhesive.

The internal chimney is made from the ceramic fibre board box section, which fits into the floor and the roof IFB brick beam. If you have difficulty obtaining this box section a chimney can be made by gluing ceramic fibre boards together.

The lid is made by gluing and pinning edge on strips of blanket onto the steel and calcium-silicate lid unit.

I have constructed my kiln in this way because it is durable and the costs are low. A similar performance kiln could be made using ceramic fibre blanket or board for the walls in place of the block.

My five cubic foot version of the power kiln has a setting space of about 1 foot 9 inches cubed. Ideal kiln shelves for this would be 1 foot 7 inches square. I have used what I had in stock, shelves one foot five inches square. Though a little on the small side, they work well.

This design is very flexible and can be built as small as two cubic feet, a setting space of one foot three inches cubed.

The kiln can also be successfully made and fired as large as fifteen cubic foot, with a setting space of two foot six inches cubed. Kilns larger than five cubic foot do require bigger jets in the burners and a bigger chimney box section.

Cost
The cost of making the power kiln will be little more than a half that of buying a similar commercially-made kiln. As new materials have to be used you cannot make the huge savings that are possible when building designs one or two with second-hand materials. The power kiln is extremely economical on fuel because of the efficiency of the new insulation materials, ceramic fibre and SAYVIT brick.

Site
With care the power kiln can be built in the workshop or garage. I have even seen such a kiln in the corner of a large kitchen. If the kiln is built on a wooden, plastic or similar floor, stand it on a sheet of asbestos or calcium-silicate. Likewise a low ceiling above the kiln should be protected. I have not heard of even a minor accident involving this type of kiln, but it pays to be safety-conscious.

1 Base bricks in place—a total of 18 whole bricks and 3 cut bricks. The burner holes are drilled with a brace and bit and enlarged to 3 inches with a pad saw and a half round file. Also a half inch deep slot is cut for the chimney box.

2 Side sheets in place to which the half inch thick fibre blanket is stuck with the special adhesive. The blanket is cut with a sharp knife. Note the $1\frac{1}{2}$ inch spyhole. Do not fit the side sheets too tightly, as they expand slightly on firing.

3 Bricklaying. The bricks are laid edge on to give a 3 inch thickness. Note the ceramic fibre paper between the bricks. This seats the bricks well. If the bricks do not fit correctly they will crack during firing.

4 With a sharp knife cut a $2\frac{1}{2}$ inch section from the chimney box.

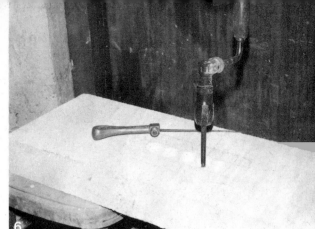

6 Cut the chimney slot in the H.T.I. roof beam. The The beam is recessed on the under side an inch to hold the chimney box.

5 Fix the chimney box into the slot in the kiln floor and cut it to the correct height. This is so that it stands one inch above the kiln walls. Two flame deflector blocks are cut from the two pieces of ceramic fibre block. These are held in place by staples made of the Kanthal wire. The wire on the hot face is covered by a thin layer of adhesive.

7 The roof beam in place. This is bedded down on a piece of 1400 grade 1 inch thick blanket.

8 Fix the calcium silicate sheet to the lid frame with one inch bolts. Cut the one inch 1400 grade blanket into 3 inch wide strips. This is fixed to the the lid with adhesive and the two steel rods which run across the lid at a depth of $1\frac{1}{2}$ inches. The rods are threaded and nuts hold them in place, when the lid has been filled with blanket. Compress as much blanket into the lid as you can. It should be $\frac{1}{2}$ inch proud at the open end of the frame. A 3-inch thickness of blanket has proved to be adequate though if I were building the kiln again I would probably afford the luxury of a slightly less hot lid with a 4 inch thickness of blanket. I have included extra 1400 grade blanket in the list of materials, for this purpose.

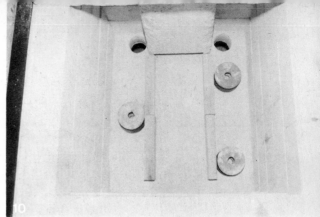

9 The lid in place butted up against the roof beam. I have stuck a 3 inch strip of 1 inch 1400 grade blanket to the edge of the roof beam, which makes for a good seal. Two handles were later fixed to the lid. Note the damper bricks.

10 The two inch deep bottom shelf supports in position. Four pieces of two inch deep brick channel the flames to the chimney.

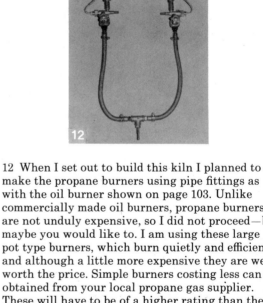

11 The bottom shelf in position. This is butted up to the chimney box, so the flames cannot take a short cut to the chimney.

12 When I set out to build this kiln I planned to make the propane burners using pipe fittings as with the oil burner shown on page 103. Unlike commercially made oil burners, propane burners are not unduly expensive, so I did not proceed—but maybe you would like to. I am using these large pot type burners, which burn quietly and efficiently, and although a little more expensive they are well worth the price. Simple burners costing less can be obtained from your local propane gas supplier. These will have to be of a higher rating than the 9000 B.T.U.'s (2.6 K.w.) each of the pot type burners. Two standard 28,000 B.T.U.'s (8.4 K.w.) blow torch burner will suffice for a five cubic foot kiln.

13 The burners clamped in position half an inch below the burner holes. I have made the burner rail adjustable on my prototype so that I could find the best position for the burners.

Firing technique for the power kiln

Compared with kilns made of traditional materials power kiln firings are very economical, using very little fuel.

The temperature rise is simply controlled by the regulator valve on the propane bottle. To start the firing the diaphragm is 'just' opened and the burners lit, which produces a slow lazy flame; during the firing this is gradually increased until at the later stages a fast powerful flame is emitted from the burner's mouth. Unlike a lot of kilns that seem to struggle up to top temperature, the power kiln fires extremely quickly, so devise a schedule that suits your pots and glazes. Fast fired glazes can work well, but the same glazes can look very different from when they are fired over a longer period.

When firing it is important that the kiln room is well ventilated. Leave a door or window wide open throughout, so that any fumes can be dispersed and the oxygen in the room is not exhausted. The first firing of the kiln will create an abnormal amount of fumes as the starch burns out of the ceramic fibre.

Another safety precaution: don't skimp on the gas tubing from the propane bottle to the burners. Buy a long length so that you can stand the bottle at least ten feet away from the kiln.

Reduction

If you would like to reduce fire, restrict the chimney by placing two pieces of $1 \times 3 \times 4\frac{1}{2}$ inch firebrick over the chimney exit on the top of the kiln. The amount the exit is restricted is critical; if closed too much the temperature will fail to rise. When optimum reduction is achieved a slight haze can be seen in the chamber. A small flame may come out of the spy hole, and a very slight glow can be seen a few inches above the chimney exit.

A pyrometer, though not essential, can make for efficient firing. Then if you over-restrict the chimney exit and the temperature fails to rise it will be indicated on the pyrometer dial. The new digital type pyrometer read-out is ideal for this as it reacts instantly. You can inch the bricks over the exit to the point where the ideal rate of temperature climb is shown.

Digital pyrometer from Podmore's Ltd.

A typical six to seven hour reduction firing in the power kiln should use about ten to twelve pounds (four to five kilos) of propane gas. Propane cannot be metered, but if the cylinder is stood on bathroom scales during the firing you can see how much gas is being used. A cylinder holding 42 lb (19 kg) of propane weighs 90 lb (41 kg) and therefore 48 lb (22 kg) when empty. For example if the cylinder weighs 80 lb (36 kg) after the first firing, 10 lb (4.5 kg) of gas has been used and you could expect three more firings from the cylinder. For further help on reduction firing see the once firing section of this book, page 73.

Left: reduction firing. A small clean flame can be seen coming out of the chimney. My pottery has a low ceiling, so as a precaution I have put a sheet of calcium silicate above the vent.

Right: unpacking the first firing. The kiln fired well, with good reduction, an overall even temperature, firing raw pots in six and a half hours to 1280°C.

Troubles and joys of kilns

It can be great fun to build a kiln and fire your own pots in it, and your sense of achievement will be doubled as your kiln will have cost you much less than you would have paid for a ready-made one.

There may be troubles, as all new kilns can be temperamental, but with thought and sometimes a little reading and research snags can be mastered.

Even with our increased understanding of modern sciences, kiln building and firing still holds many mysteries, and firing a new kiln is done with great trepidation. This is why, throughout the world, kiln firing is shrouded in ritual and superstition, with many offerings and prayers to the gods. My last kiln was commissioned with a bottle of wine and my fingers crossed.

4 Wheel building

There are many types of potters' wheels available, but for this book I have chosen three, which are relatively easy to make, for which parts and materials are readily available, and whose basic designs are preferred by the majority of practising studio potters. The three are a traditional cranked kick wheel, a momentum or continental wheel, and an electric wheel, powered by a D.C. motor with the speed controlled by a variable transformer.

I chose the traditional cranked kick wheel because generations of British potters have learnt to throw on it. It is highly thought of and well proven. If I were limited to one wheel in my pottery I would choose this type without hesitation.

The momentum wheel is easy and inexpensive to make and once mastered is a delight to use.

The D.C. variable speed electric wheel with its very wide range of running speeds and sensitive speed control can mimic the properties of the kick wheel. For this reason and because it is powerful and quiet at all speeds, it is the only wheel that would tempt many potters away from their kick wheel.

I have seen some good electric wheels which have been built very inexpensively using the ring-cone and double-cone principles, but to make these wheels a high degree of engineering skill is required. They are also made of components that are not easily available. Unlike the D.C. variable speed wheel, even the best of these would not have altered my preference for the cranked kick wheel.

Metric measurements for wheels
The transition from imperial to metric measurements is causing difficulty in the lumber and engineering trades, so; on the wheel plans I quote both systems of measurements. I have not done this in the text as I feel

it will clutter the page and confuse the reader.

One inch = 2.54 centimetres.

One foot = 30.48 centimetres.

In the lumber trade the conversion is often done at 2.5 centimetres to the inch.

Figure 12 Side view of the kickwheel.

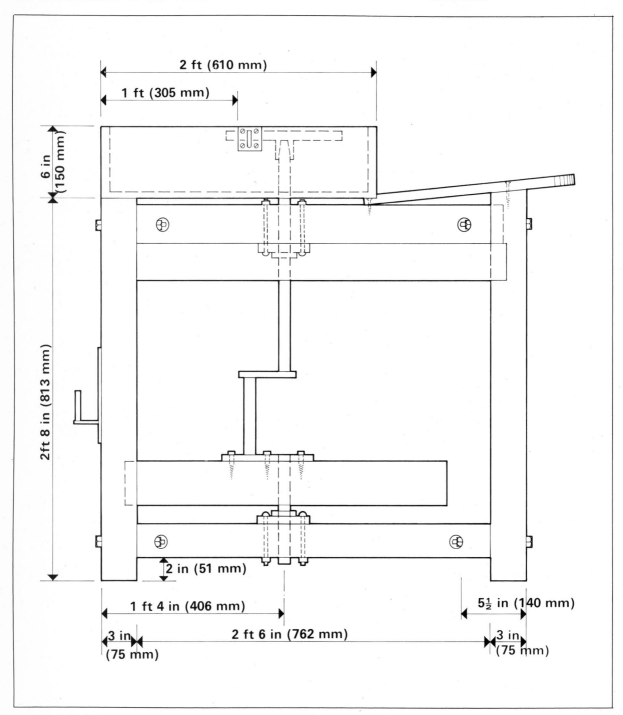

Kick wheel

The height of the kick bar on this wheel is adjustable, which makes it suitable for most people. If the thrower is very small or extremely tall the overall dimensions can be adjusted without detriment to the wheel.

You may save a lot of money if you are able to find good quality second-hand lumber, but no compromise should be made when making the shaft, which should be made to the highest standards. If the shaft is badly aligned the wheel head will oscillate.

Flywheel

The standard flywheel is 2 ft 4 inches wide and 4 inches

Figure 13 Kickwheel, viewed from overhead position.

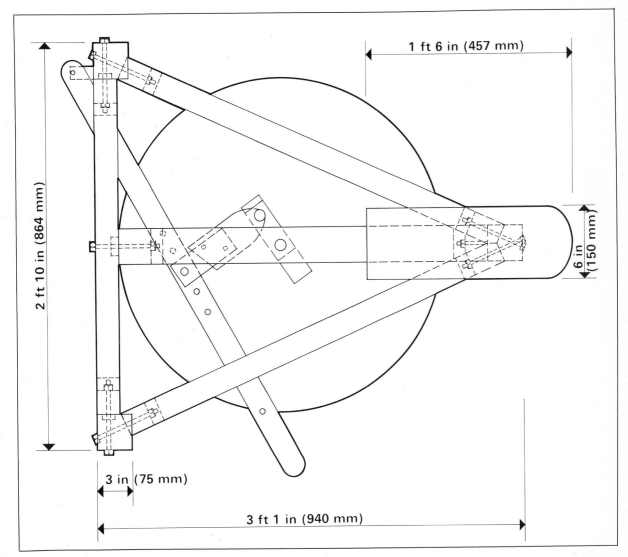

deep. It should be made of planks glued and screwed at right angles to each other. Use the cheapest lumber available. If a heavy flywheel is required make it deeper and/or add lead weights to the outer rim.

This makes an average weight flywheel. The dimensions can be altered depending on your requirements. If you normally make large quantities of small pots I would recommend the lighter flywheel. A heavier flywheel is more suitable for making larger pots.

A hollow flywheel that can be filled with varying amounts of ballast can easily be constructed. (See Fig. 14.) This has the advantage of enabling you to

Figure 14 A flywheel with adjustable weight, for the kickwheel.

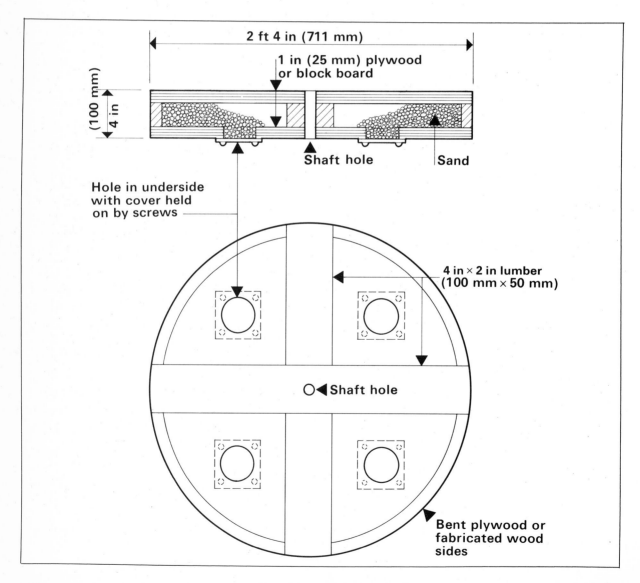

experiment and choose an ideal weight of flywheel which suits you and the type of ware that you are making. For making quantities of small pots a light flywheel is an advantage as a heavy one has too much momentum and continually stopping and starting it can be tiring. When making large pots a heavy flywheel is an advantage as its greater momentum gives smooth slow running with less kicking, which is ideal for the more lengthy process of making large ware.

This flywheel should be made as shown in Fig. 14. The side can be made from a strip of thin plywood. This is soaked in water so it can easily be bent to shape. If a bandsaw is available the side can be laminated from short pieces of wood glued together. When the glue is dry the whole flywheel is cut to shape including the top and bottom panels.

Shaft

The shaft is made of 1 inch round steel as shown in Fig. 15. A local small engineering works, blacksmith or agricultural engineer are the ideal people to make the metal work for this wheel.

The shaft joints should be welded whilst the shaft is turning slowly, so the weld is even and no stresses are set up in the metal. The shaft is made with section R in place which is only removed after all the welding has been completed. The shaft's crank is off-set by 3 inches, which gives a smooth fairly fast running wheel head. If this is decreased by up to $\frac{3}{4}$ inch it will run faster; if it is increased by up to 1 inch the wheel will run slower. However, the 3 inch offset suits most people. The plates (see S on Fig. 15) are 2 inches wide.

The wheel head fitting, M in Fig. 15, is a no. 3 Morse taper. The other standard fittings are a $\frac{3}{4}$ inch Whitworth screw and 20 mm continental screw. (In the U.S. there is no such standardized taper and the cost for milling one would be exorbitant. It is possible to use standard set screws alone as wheel head fittings.)

Kick bar bracket C
This is made of $2 \times \frac{1}{4}$ inch angle iron. It has three screw holes in it by which it is attached to the leg of the wheel. It has a split pin $\frac{1}{2}$ inch from the top of the peg. This is to retain the kick bar.

Shaft, crank connector and leather strip, kick bar bracket, hook and chain, bearings and hardwood wheel head. Note that on the crank of the shaft there is an adjustable sleeve. This is not essential but it helps keep the crank connector in place.

Crank connector D plus A, B and L

The crank connector is made of a 2×3 inch piece of wood and is held onto the kick bar by metal plates A and B. A $\frac{1}{2} \times 3\frac{1}{2}$ inch long carriage bolt passes through the large holes on plates A and B, and through the kick bar. The attachment to the kick bar can be made adjustable by drilling several holes in the kick bar. Eight holes at 2 inch intervals, the first one being 4 inches from the kick bar pivot peg will give the wheel a range of kicking actions. Depending on the height and build of the thrower, one of these holes will prove to be suitable. The connector is held onto the shaft's crank by a strip of leather, Part L, by two screws or bolts (see Fig. 15).

Figure 15 Tray, shaft and metal work for the kickwheel.

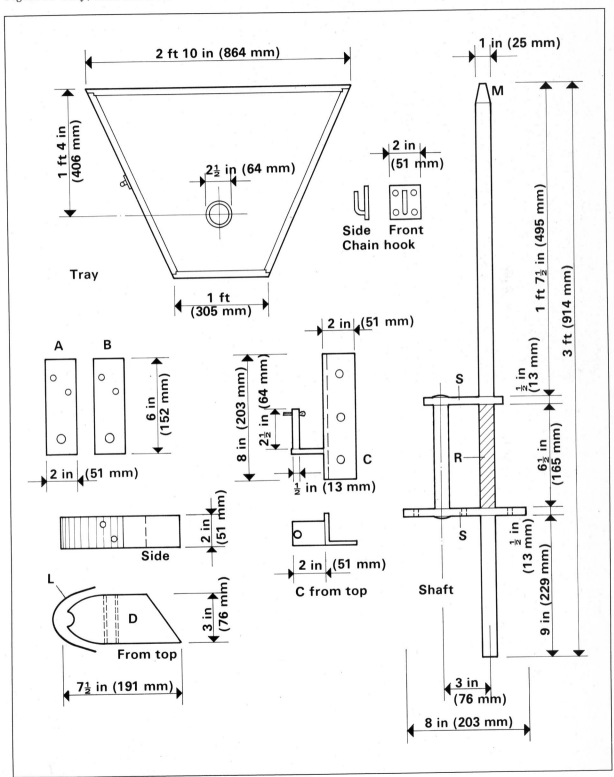

Assembly notes

A Cut all wood for frame (except cross-rail) and cut tenon joints where applicable.

B Cut mortice joints.

C Assemble frame. For a very rigid and permanent fixture the joints can be glued and dowelled. If you wish the wheel to be taken apart at a future date the joints should be left dry and carriage bolts used to secure them. For some parts it may be more convenient to use lag bolts. When finished the wheel is 2 ft 10 inches wide. If it will not pass through your door frame the joints are best left dry and carriage-bolted.

D Cut $1\frac{1}{2}$ inch holes for the shaft in the top and bottom rails, fit bottom bearing and put shaft in position.

E Make and put flywheel in position.

F Lag bolt flywheel to shaft and tighten bottom bearing onto shaft.

G Fit top bearing and tighten onto shaft.

H Make and fit the kick bar and bracket. (See metal work notes on making crank connector, page 122.)

I Fit cross-rail to frame. The cross-rail is fitted to the left-hand side of the wheel from the top back of the wheel to the bottom front (seat end).
It should be cut to size and lag bolted onto the frame. This cross-rail gives extra rigidity to the frame.

J Make tray. This is pinned and glued with water-proof glue, and is painted on the inside with at least four coats of water-proof polyurethane varnish or hard gloss paint.

K Fit seat and tray to frame. The tray can either be screwed to the frame, or be made removable by fixing two stops to the underside of it. These butt up against the end legs, and a small door bolt is fitted to complete the fixing.

L Lubricate and paint.

Materials

Wood—either a good softwood or hardwood
　Frame comprises:
　　5 lengths planed of 3×3 inch $\times$ 3 ft
　　7 lengths planed of 3×2 inch $\times$ 3 ft
　　1 length planed of 3×2 inch $\times$ 4 ft
Sides of the tray
　　1 length of 6×1 inch $\times$ 10 ft
　　Base of tray (see Fig. 15)
　　12 mm resin bonded plywood
Seat
　　1 length of $6 \times 1\frac{1}{2}$ inch $\times$ 1 ft 6 inches
　　Wood for flywheel
Metal work comprising:
　　Shaft
　　Kick bar bracket
　　Crank connector
　　Hook for chain
　　2 ft 6 inches of 1 inch linked chain
　　14 carriage bolts, $6 \times \frac{3}{8}$ inch
　　10 lag bolts $3 \times \frac{3}{8}$ inch
　　1 wheel head
　　$2\frac{1}{2}$–5 inch plastic drain pipe
　　2 self-aligning 1 inch bearings
　　1 small door bolt
　　Strip of leather 7×2 inches (for crank connector)
　　A few screws, varnish, paint

The sequence of photographs shows Medway College of Design ceramic students constructing a kickwheel.

1–4 Assembling the frame. The mortice and tenon joints should fit tightly. The joints are carriage bolted, which means the wheel can be taken apart.

5 Filling the adjustable weight flywheel with ballast. Most potters like a heavy flywheel.

6 Completing the wheel by fixing the seat, bearings, shaft and flywheel.

7 The completed wheel, with its kickboard and crank connector. For this wheel we made a metal and hardwood connector; the leather and wood connector is easier to make and works as well. The wheel was completed with a turned hardwood wheel head. A local engineer turned a small metal shank to fit the head on the shaft. The tray was painted with several coats of polyurethane varnish.

Continental wheel

This is a much less sophisticated structure than the cranked kick wheel and can be made relatively cheaply using second-hand lumber. I have known potters who have built this wheel for just the cost of a bag of cement, a few screws and a wheel-head, the rest of the materials having been found or given to them.

The dimensions and gauges of the wood can be varied to suit your needs, and according to the lumber that is available. The requirements are that the structure should be rigid and it should 'fit' the thrower.

The wheel frame should be assembled according to the basic plans which can be adjusted to suit your requirements. For example, a splash tray can be added. Another useful adaption that can easily be made is an adjustable seat, which should be made so that the seat can be moved forward as well as up and down. The whole structure is held together by screws or lag bolts. screws.

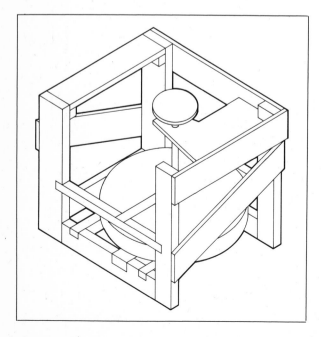

Figure 16 The continental wheel.

Assembly notes for flywheel

1 Drill a $1\frac{1}{2}$ inch hole in the centre of the circular piece of chipboard/plywood and also in the centre of the $8 \times 8 \times 4$ inch piece of softwood.
2 Screw the block of wood to the centre of the chipboard.
3 Knock the nails in all over the chipboard at 3 inch intervals, leaving them 2 to $2\frac{1}{2}$ inches proud. These are to strengthen the concrete.
4 Pin the 4 inch strip of hardboard round the circumference of the chipboard.
5 Fill with concrete. This should be made of one part cement and six parts concrete aggregate.
6 The cement should be thoroughly tamped down and when it has almost set it should be lightly tamped to produce small ridges radiating from the centre. These give purchase to the foot when kicking.
7 When the concrete is set the flywheel can be slipped into the framework of the wheel and the shaft set into the flywheel and attached by screwing the steel plate to the centre block by four $\frac{3}{8} \times 2\frac{1}{2}$ inch coach screws.

Materials

1 circular piece of 1 inch thick chipboard/
  plywood (2 ft 6 inches diameter)
1 block of softwood $8 \times 8 \times 4$ inches
100 3 inch round headed nails.
8 lag bolts, $\frac{3}{8} \times 3$ inches
1 inch self-aligning bearing for bottom
$1\frac{1}{2}$ inch self-aligning bearing or plumber block
  for top
1 piece of hard board 4 inches $\times$ 8 ft
Shaft as shown in Fig. 21
$\frac{1}{2}$ bag of cement and 2 cwt concrete aggregate
Wood and screws suitable for
making wheel frame

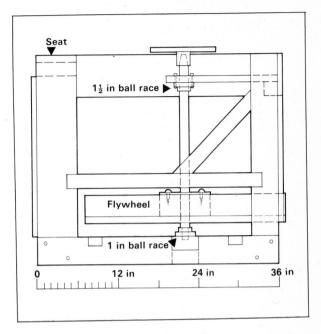

Figure 17 Continental wheel, seen from the right,
cross section.

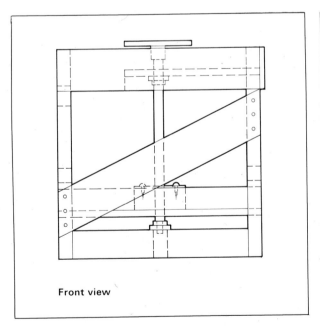

Figure 18 Continental wheel, viewed from front.

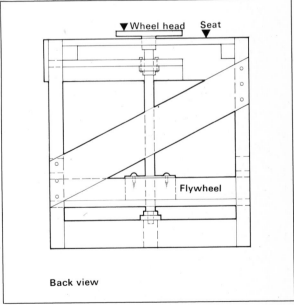

Figure 19 Continental wheel, viewed from back.

127

Making the flywheel for the continental wheel.

The base, showing the side wall which retains the concrete. Note the use of nails to strengthen and bond the concrete to the base.

The base, filled with concrete. Note the tamped foothold ridges on the concrete.

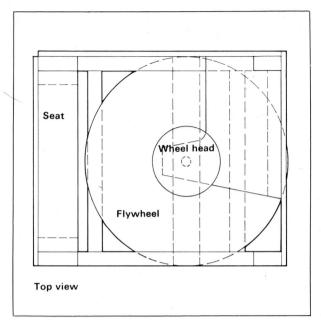

Seat

Wheel head

Flywheel

Top view

Figure 20 Continental wheel, viewed from overhead.

Figure 21 (below): Continental wheel, the flywheel and shaft.

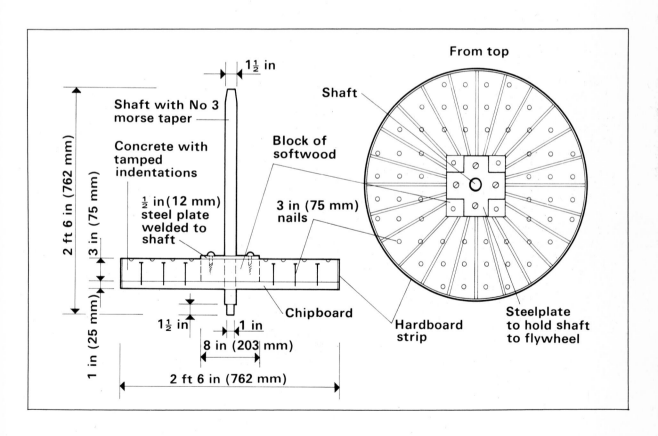

From top

$1\frac{1}{2}$ in

Shaft

Shaft with No 3 morse taper

Block of softwood

Concrete with tamped indentations

$\frac{1}{2}$ in (12 mm) steel plate welded to shaft

3 in (75 mm) nails

2 ft 6 in (762 mm)

3 in (75 mm)

1 in (25 mm)

Chipboard

$1\frac{1}{2}$ in

1 in

8 in (203 mm)

2 ft 6 in (762 mm)

Hardboard strip

Steelplate to hold shaft to flywheel

129

Power wheel—variable transformer type

I have used most types of electric wheel and have found this one is by far the most useful for the average pottery. This wheel gets its wide speed range, power and smooth silent running from a $\frac{1}{3}$ h.p. D.C. motor, which is fed from a variable voltage transformer. This is the most expensive component of the wheel. Try to find a good second-hand motor, or an inexpensive one from a services surplus supply store—a little perseverance will be needed as they are less abundant than A.C. motors. An ex-naval captain living in our village pointed out to me that ships use D.C. electricity and a fruitful source of quality D.C. electric motors are ship-breaking yards. He obtained for me a beautifully made heavy-duty motor, which is now installed in one of my wheels.

Using a very rough estimate, making the wheel with a second-hand or surplus stock motor should cost you about one-third of the price of an equivalent wheel sold by the pottery supplier. If you have to buy a new motor, your wheel will cost you about two-thirds of a commercially-made wheel. One way of reducing the expense would be to replace the speed control transformer with a thyristor control. Wheels have been built on this principle, but I have not generally found them reliable or robust enough for my purposes.

This is basically the wheel described in the instructions and plans for the power wheel. One or two minor differences can be seen in the photograph, such as the seat support.

Materials

Body
1 sheet 12 mm × 8 × 4 ft resin bonded plywood
10 ft of 2 × 2 inch softwood
6 ft of 2 × 1 inch softwood
50 1½ inch wood screws
Large tube of whitewood glue

Motor
D.C. motor ⅓ h.p.
5A Frame 220 volt, 2.5 amp.
2000 R.P.M. continuous rating, shunt wound, enclosed
(The motor must have a bearing suitable for working in a vertical position.)
In the U.S. available new from: Applied Motors, Inc. 4801 Boeing Dr., Rockford, IL 61109 or Graham Transmissions, Inc., P.O. Box 160, Menomonee Falls, WI 53051.
See notes on fitting components p. 134.

Metal work
Shaft ⅞ inch round steel 2 ft 3 inches long, with no. 3 morse taper at top
Motor mounting brackets
2 inch 'A' belt pulley with the same bore as the shaft of the motor
12 inch 'A' belt pulley, ⅞ inch bore
'A' belt from motor pulley to main pulley (the length of the belt is measured by wrapping a piece of thin string round the 2 inch motor pulley to the 12 inch drive pulley)
2 bearings, ⅞ inch self-aligning
Carriage bolts—the size and quantity will depend on the type and size of the motor and bearings for which they are used

D.C. motor speed controller: *Alternative 1*
Regospeed D.C. motor controller

Regospeed

TYPE HSR	402.62
Supply voltage	200–250 v 50 Hz
Armature current	2.0 A.rms dc
Field current	1.0 A.rms dc

Available from: Claude Lyons Ltd, Ware Road, Hoddesdon, Herts.
If you obtain a D.C. shunt wound motor of a different specification, a different model of controller will be required. Consult the manufacturer or an electrician. (See notes on speed controller, page 134.)

Note: In the U.S. this motor controller is called a rheostat.

D.C. motor speed controller: *Alternative 2*
Components to make the speed control unit (see notes, page 134).
Thin steel plate 21 × 6 inches for chassis (see Fig. 26
Variable speed transformer no. 404, available from Claude Lyons Ltd, address above.
2 silicon rectifiers no. 44 low voltage 280 v rms 2.5 A D.C.
Components as shown in Figure 25
1 1¼ inch pulley (see Fig. 26)

Foot control (see Fig. 27)
34 ½ inch round steel rods
5 1 inch round steel rods
2 ½ inch plumber block bearings
4 ¼ × 1½ inch long bolts
1 ¼ × 3 inch long bolt and nut
Aircraft control cable 2 ft long
5 inch steel spring of approximately ½ inch diameter

This wheel has an identical specification to the one described in the text, but has a much more sophisticated cabinet. This was made from small offcuts of African hardwood, a material which was readily available to me and it produced a handsome and practical body. The basic electrical and control system for this wheel is very flexible and was very easily fitted into the compact cabinet.

Constructing the power wheel

The first stage in making this wheel is to make the wooden body (Figs. 22–3 should be self-explanatory). If made with an adjustable seat the dimensions of the wheel should suit most potters' requirements, but as this system is easily adapted it can be made to suit almost any potter's needs.

Cut the plywood as indicated on the cutting plan (Fig. 22). The excess plywood from the plywood sheet can be used to make a shelf for the back of the wheel.

The top of the wheel body should be made so it is easily removable, which allows it to be serviced easily. An equally good alternative for constructing this wheel is to fix the motor on the left-hand side, near the back of the body. This allows the back panel to be removed, which makes servicing the wheel a little more difficult, but you may find that if the top is glued and firmly screwed on water and dirt are less likely to penetrate the workings.

On completing the body of the wheel, including fitting the base and top bearing supports, a $1\frac{1}{2}$ inch hole should be drilled in the centre of both top bearing supports and the base. These are to accommodate the bearings and shaft.

Figure 22 Cutting plan for the body of the electric wheel, from a plywood sheet 12 mm thick, size 8×4 ft (240×120 cm).

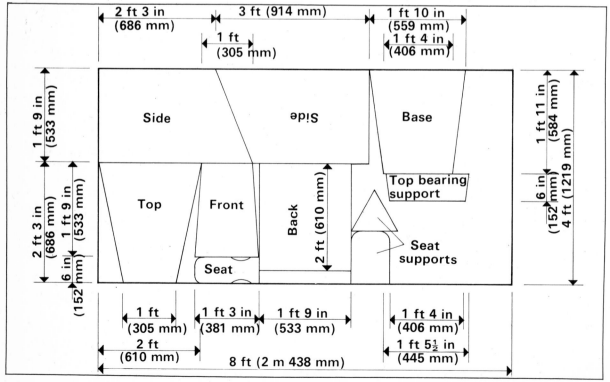

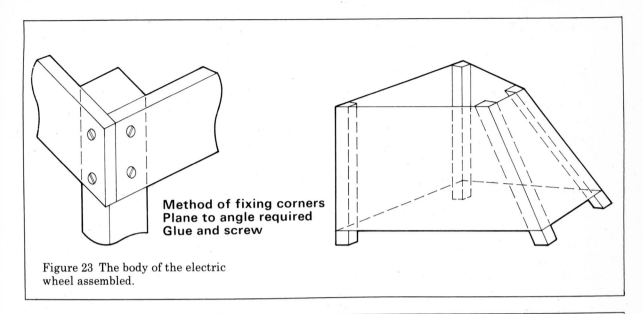

Method of fixing corners
Plane to angle required
Glue and screw

Figure 23 The body of the electric
wheel assembled.

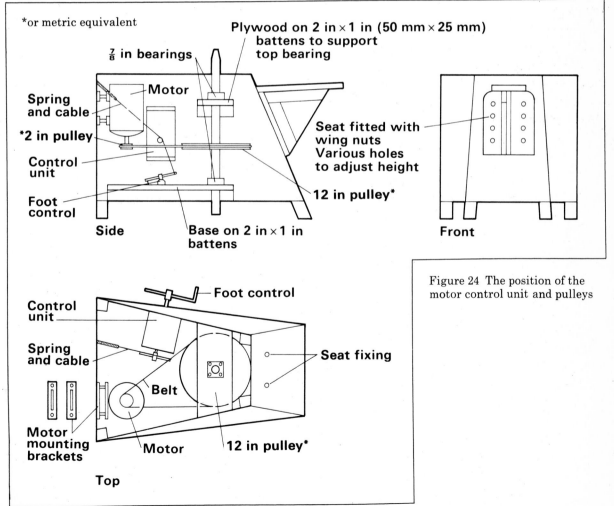

*or metric equivalent

$\frac{7}{8}$ in bearings

Plywood on 2 in × 1 in (50 mm × 25 mm)
battens to support
top bearing

Motor

Spring
and cable

*2 in pulley

Control
unit

Foot
control

Side

Base on 2 in × 1 in
battens

Seat fitted with
wing nuts
Various holes
to adjust height

12 in pulley*

Front

Figure 24 The position of the
motor control unit and pulleys

Control
unit

Foot control

Spring
and cable

Seat fixing

Belt

Motor
mounting
brackets

Motor

12 in pulley*

Top

Fitting components

After completing the body, start to fit it out by installing the motor, bearings, shaft and pulleys, as shown in Fig. 24. The motor should be hung on adjustable brackets, the size and design of which will depend on the dimensions of the mounting plates of the electric motor. The purpose of these brackets is to allow the motor to slide horizontally, enabling the belt to be tensioned. To minimise any motor vibration, rubber washers or rubber pads are placed between the motor and the mounting brackets.

If you are unable to find a motor of the indicated specification, a $\frac{1}{4}$ or $\frac{1}{2}$ h.p. motor can be an adequate replacement, but the other electronic components will have to be adjusted accordingly. The speed of the motor is not critical. Motors of 800 r.p.m. and 1400 r.p.m. can often be found and are good substitutes as long as the other specifications are similar.

Your local small engineering works, agricultural engineers, or blacksmith will be able to make the shaft and motor mounting brackets. They should also be able to supply the pulleys, bearings, carriage bolts and the 'A' belt.

The shaft is long enough to enable you to set it at a height which you find most comfortable for throwing.

Speed control unit

Alternative 1: The speed controller can be purchased as a complete unit on its chassis. A sensible safety precaution would be to fix a thermal or magnetic cut-out between the unit and the power supply.

Alternative 2: If you are a competent electrician it is well worthwhile wiring the speed control unit. A large saving can be made by purchasing the separate components and wiring them as shown in Fig. 25 opposite. However, if you have to employ an electrician to do this the total cost of the unit would be very similar to the ready-made unit. **If your electrical knowledge is scanty do not attempt to assemble this unit. Not only could it be dangerous but any small error could cause expensive damage to either the motor, rectifiers or transformer.**

Further savings can be made if you are going to make up the speed controller, as second-hand variable

Figure 25 The electrical circuit.

Figure 26 Electric wheel, the speed control unit.

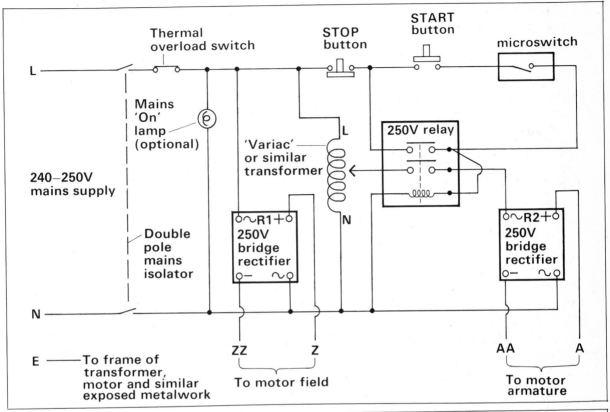

Thermal overload switch

STOP button

START button

microswitch

L

Mains 'On' lamp (optional)

'Variac' or similar transformer

L

250V relay

240–250V mains supply

Double pole mains isolator

~R1+ 250V bridge rectifier

– ~

N

~R2+ 250V bridge rectifier

– ~

N

ZZ   Z

AA   A

E — To frame of transformer, motor and similar exposed metalwork

To motor field

To motor armature

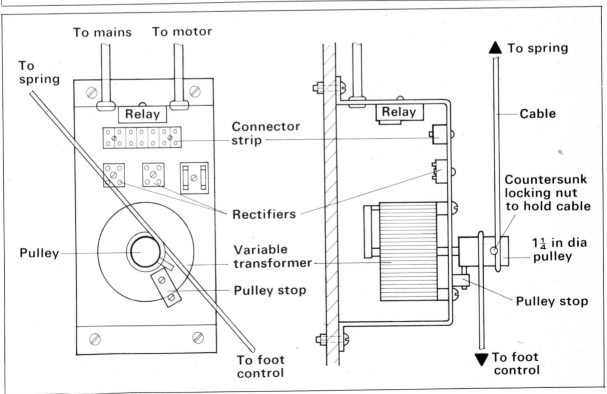

To mains   To motor

To spring

Relay

Relay

To spring

Cable

Connector strip

To spring

Rectifiers

Countersunk locking nut to hold cable

Pulley

Variable transformer

$1\frac{1}{4}$ in dia pulley

Pulley stop

Pulley stop

To foot control

To foot control

transformers are available, but these are easily damaged. Check that the copper winding which surrounds the outside is unmarked, as any break in the winding renders the unit useless. Enquire about the transformer when looking for a suitable shunt wound D.C. motor. The transformer's speed control shaft is operated from a small $1\frac{1}{4}$ inch pulley (see Fig. 26, previous page). If you cannot buy this pulley it can be turned out of aluminium. Alternatively, a $1\frac{3}{4}$ inch 'A' belt pulley will suffice.

The wheel can be wired direct to the main power supply, but for ease of operation and safety an ON/OFF push button and a microswitch should be installed. The microswitch can be attached to the control box, so that when the pulley stop comes to rest it also contacts the microswitch (see Fig. 26). Another suitable place for the microswitch is under the foot control's swing arm, so that when the foot control is in the 'off' position it comes to rest on the microswitch.

The ON/OFF push button assembly should be placed on the side of the wheel that easily comes to hand. By far the best type is the assembly which is covered by a plastic membrane so that it is completely water-tight.

The microswitch is positioned so as to be operated (and its contacts closed) only when the variable transformer is set to zero. The START button is therefore only effective at the transformer's zero setting.

The relay has a 240–250 v coil and two sets of normally open contacts. One set is used to provide a hold-on supply to the relay coil. The other set is used to connect the tap of the variable transformer to the rectifier feeding the armature of the motor.

The START button is closed when pushed, whereas the STOP button is normally closed and open when pushed. The arrangement of the two buttons and the microswitch, controlling the relay, makes the wheel very safe in use.

The overload device has to be selected to suit the size of the motor but provides very useful protection for the circuit. If it is omitted, a fuse should be provided.

Safety note
D.C. ELECTRICITY KILLS! When servicing or
installing the variable speed unit and the motor,
always have the wheel unplugged from the mains
supply. Unless you are a very competent electrician,
get the wiring for the speed control unit, ON/OFF
switch, microswitch and thermal/magnetic cut-out
done professionally. These are only small jobs and the
cost should be minimal. Please re-read the notes on
speed control unit, above.

Foot control unit
If you do not have a tap to thread the steel parts it can
be done for little cost at any small engineering
establishment. The foot control is installed on the
wheel floor, and then fix the speed control unit into the
wheel body. The 5 inch spring should be secured by a
screw or hook to the back of the wheel, as in Fig. 27
page 138. The cable is attached to the spring, wound
twice round the control box pulley and fixed to the
swing arm of the foot control. The foot control and the
length of the cable should be adjusted so that when the
foot control is at rest, the spring is under minimum
tension and the rotating arm of the transformer in the
control box is in the 'off' position. When all is adjusted
to your satisfaction the cable should be locked onto the
control box pulley by means of the locking nut.

Finishing the body
Fix a heel rest; it should be comfortably positioned on
the right-hand side of the wheel. On my wheel I have
done this by screwing on a block of wood. If several
potters are going to use the wheel you may wish to
make the heel rest adjustable.

At this stage a shelf at the back of the wheel to take
a board of pots may be added, or a tool box.

The wheel is now ready for sanding and painting. If
you have chosen a plywood with a nice veneer on it
this can be enhanced by several coats of polyurethane
varnish, which gives a very durable finish.

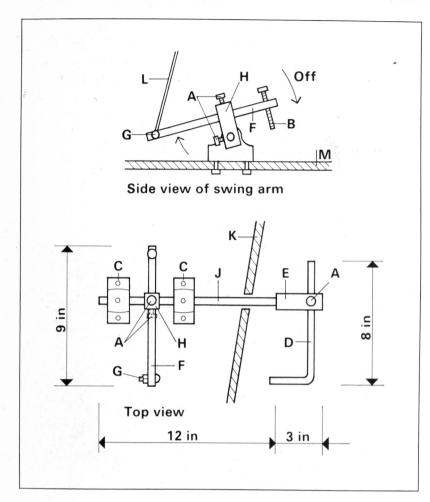

Figure 27 The foot control.

A ¼ inch (8 mm) bolts tapped into parts to hold unit together
B ¼ inch (8 mm) bolt as an adjustable stop
C Plumber block bearings
D Foot pedal, ½ inch (12 mm) round steel bar, which is pressed down to start
E 1 × 1 × 3 inch (25 × 25 × 75 mm) steel block to hold foot pedal
F Swing arm, made of ½ inch (12 mm) round steel bar
G ¼ inch bolt with a hole in it to hold cable
H 1 × 1 × 2 inch (25 × 25 × 50 mm) block to hold swing arm
J Centre pivot, made of ½ inch (12 mm) steel bar
K Wooden right hand side of wheel
L Cable to control box pulley
M Wooden base

The tray

The last job is to make a tray for the wheel. The size depends very much on your potting habits—personally I like a big tray. The tray can be made out of wood, which will require at least four coats of waterproof polyurethane or hard gloss paint to make it waterproof. Some commercial wheel manufacturers will supply plastic or fibreglass trays at a reasonable price.

The trays on the wheels in the photographs (see pp. 130–131) were made of fibre glass. The fibre glass matt and resin comes complete with instructions. The larger of the two trays was made by borrowing a tray for a day from a friend's wheel, which was used as a mould. I found making it this way very quick and easy —the only slight problem I had was that I found my tray a little reluctant to come away from the original, which I had not cleaned and prepared sufficiently.

In the case of the smaller tray I made my own mould, constructed of several blocks of wood, which were screwed together and roughly cut to shape. A smooth surface was achieved by using a power drill sanding disc and plenty of plastic filler.

With both these trays I set locating pins into the fibre on the underside, so that the tray sat firmly on the wheel body but could easily be removed for cleaning.

Making simple tools

Steel required to make turning tools can be purchased for a fraction of the cost of the finished product. I make mine by heating the steel with a blow torch and bending it into shape over a small hearth made of firebrick. The tool is then shaped by filing. A grinding wheel can take the hard work out of this operation. The blow torch can also be used for firing the small kiln, too.

This photograph shows some of the everyday tools that I use in my workshop which can be made very cheaply. A little innovation in the pottery will save you a great deal of money.
A Whirler or banding wheel: the top was made from a circular piece of hardwood. The base was made from a square piece of plywood. Between them I have fastened a second-hand two piece bearing.
B Throwing gauge, as shown in Figure 28.
C Another type of throwing gauge: this was made from a tin, filled with cement, in which the upright steel rod was set. A horizontal gauge rod is held onto the upright by means of a stout rubber band.

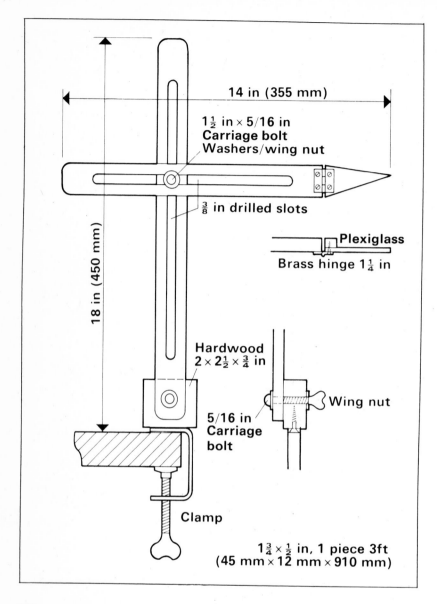

14 in (355 mm)

$1\frac{1}{2}$ in × 5/16 in
Carriage bolt
Washers/wing nut

$\frac{3}{8}$ in drilled slots

Plexiglass

Brass hinge $1\frac{1}{4}$ in

18 in (450 mm)

Hardwood
$2 × 2\frac{1}{2} × \frac{3}{4}$ in

Wing nut

5/16 in
Carriage
bolt

Clamp

$1\frac{3}{4} × \frac{1}{2}$ in, 1 piece 3ft
(45 mm × 12 mm × 910 mm)

Figure 28 For making repetition
ware a useful addition to any
wheel is a throwing gauge.
Here is a design that is easily and
inexpensively made.

When I set up my pottery I had a consuming desire
to make pots, some potting skill and very little else. I
was forced to be a self-reliant potter and I was
continually surprised by what could be achieved with
minimal skills.

Pottery is the complete craft, as it exploits every
aspect of a person's ability, practical and aesthetic.
Very few hobbies or occupations demand and give so
much. The complete potter must be a resourceful artist,
chemist, artisan, and much more. If you can in some
way achieve this balance, you will find real fulfillment
as a potter.

Book list

I have listed here publications for further reading about subjects covered in this book.

Glaze chemistry is a large and fascinating subject and can be approached on many different levels. I hope that the section on understanding glazes in this book will get you hooked, and you will go on to delve into works such as *Clay and Glazes for the Potter* and *Pioneer Pottery*.

No one work can cover the subject of kiln design, and *Kiln Building* and *The Kiln Book* are invaluable.

Clay and Glazes for the Potter
Daniel Rhodes (Chilton/A. & C. Black)
This has become the studio potter's standard work on glaze chemistry. I hope that the Understanding Glazes section of my book will give newcomers to this subject the confidence to tackle such books.

Oriental Glazes Nigel Wood (Watson-Guptill/A. & C. Black)
Nigel Wood describes in a very personal way the construction and qualities of the various stoneware and porcelain Eastern glazes. His view of glaze chemistry contrasts with that of Daniel Rhodes.

Pioneer Pottery Michael Cardew (Longman)
A book for the truly independent potter, reflecting Michael Cardew's personal view of the craft. His book covers in depth clay, glazes, kilns, geology, equipment and much more. I suspect the average newcomer to potting would find his chemistry very intimidating, but perseverance will bring rewards.

Salt Glazed Ceramics Jack Troy (Watson-Guptill/Pitman)
This is an excellent guide to all aspects of salt glazing. During salt glaze firing toxic and corrosive gases are given off, and human and animal life as well as the kiln can be put in danger. With knowledge and care, though, one can go on to exploit the beauties of salt glazed ware.

Ceramic Glazes Singer and German (published by Borax Consolidated Ltd, Borax House, Carlisle Place, London SW1, and obtainable direct from them)
This book gives the formula for most types of earthenware and stoneware glazes. Useful further reading after Daniel Rhodes *Clay and Glazes for the Potter*

Ceramic Glazes Cullen W. Parmelee (Cahners)
A tome which is not to be read cover to cover. It was written for the ceramic industry, but can be an invaluable reference book for the craft potter.

A Potter's Guide to Raw Glazing and Oil Firing Dennis Parks (Scribners/A. & C. Black)
Dennis Parks describes in detail the alternative method of raw glazing. He glazes his ware bone dry. The oil firing section is very useful; he describes how to fire kilns by free waste-oil (sump oil).

Kiln Building Ian Gregory
(Watson Guptill/A. & C. Black)
If you wish to build a more
ambitious wood, oil, or gas-fired
kiln than the ones I describe,
Ian Gregory's book is an ideal
starting point.

The Kiln Book (second edition)
Frederick Olsen (Chilton)
This work is packed full of
detailed kiln information. The
author gives full details of the
Olsen Fastfire Wood Kiln,
which is a twin firebox version
of my Kiln Design 1, the
through-draught kiln. Because
of the kiln's efficiency it has
become very popular; its
excellent design enables it to be
fired up to 1300°C in less than
four hours. Some Olsen kiln
owners make firing a race,
with the quality of the finished
pots being secondary; the
subtleties of wood firing
(toasting and flashing) can be
lost this way. In a very fast
efficient firing not enough wood
is burnt to create a good flow
of fly-ash over the pots. If you
use Olsen's design, develop a
firing schedule that suits your
ware, whether it be fast or
medium firing.

*Geology of the Country around
Okehampton* (HMSO
publications, London)
This detailed study of my area's
geology has proved invaluable
for my clay and glaze research.
Ask at your library or
bookshop, as they probably
have a survey of your area's
landscape.

The Craft of the Potter Michael
Casson (BBC Publications)
The ideal introduction to the
craft.

Ceramic Review, bi-monthly
magazine of the Craftsmen
Potters Association, William
Blake House, Marshall Street,
London W1.
Written by potters for potters.
Over a period of time the whole
spectrum of ceramic technique
is covered.

Pottery Quarterly, edited by
Murray Fieldhouse, Northfield
Studios, Tring, Herts.
The alternative to *Ceramic
Review*. Interesting, lively but
not quarterly.

Studio Potter, Box 65,
Goffstown, NH 03045, bi-yearly.
Technical magazine, edited by
potters, produced by potters,
including process, equipment,
production procedures, profiles
of craftsmen.

Ceramics Monthly, Box 12448,
Columbus, OH 43212, 10 times
per year. Technical articles,
portfolios, activities review.

Temperature conversion chart

Degrees Centigrade	to	Degrees Fahrenheit
50		122
100		212
200		392
300		572
400		752
500		932
600		1112
700		1292
800		1472
900		1652
1000		1832
1050		1922
1100		2012
1150		2102
1200		2192
1300		2372
1350		2462
1400		2552

Index